MAÑANA

Christian Theology
from a Hispanic Perspective

Justo L. González

ABINGDON PRESS
Nashville

MAÑANA:
CHRISTIAN THEOLOGY FROM A HISPANIC PERSPECTIVE

Copyright © 1990 by Abingdon Press

Library of Congress Cataloging-in-Publication Data
González, Justo L., 1937–
   Mañana: Christian Theology from a Hispanic Perspective. / Justo L. González
      p.   cm.
   ISBN 0-687-23067-5 (alk. paper)
      1. Theology, Doctrinal—United States.   2. Hispanic Americans—Religion.
   3. Liberation Theology. I. Title
BT30.U6665   230'.08968073—dc20   90-36110

Scripture excerpts are from the Revised Standard Version of the Bible, copyright 1946, 1952, 1971 by the Division of Christian Education of the National Council of Churches of Christ in the USA. Used by permission.

Excerpts from "El Profeta del Barrio" by Carlos Rosas reprinted by permission of the Mexican American Cultural Center.

04 05 06 07 08 09—19 18 17 16 15 14

Printed in the United States of America on recycled, acid-free paper.

MAÑANA

Christian Theology
from a Hispanic Perspective

CONTENTS

ACKNOWLEDGEMENTS

Those to whom I am indebted in the preparation of this book are too numerous to mention. As I say in the text itself—in the section in chapter 1 on "Fuenteovejuna Theology"—most of them I do not even know by name. Many are ancient Christian writers who have now been my companions in life for over three decades. Others are colleagues and friends, both in this country and throughout the world, whose writings and conversations have taught me much.

Still, there are some who deserve special mention. Part of this book, in an earlier stage of development, was read and discussed by members of a course at Perkins School of Theology. Much of it has profited from discussion among the Hispanic Instructors of Perkins, in the United Methodist Roundtable of Ethnic Minority Theologians, and in other such circles. Part of it has been published in *Apuntes*, or in a study that I conducted for the Fund for Theological Education, Inc., under the title of *The Theological Education of Hispanics;* and to those who have commented on such publications I am also grateful. My secretary, Mr. Javier Quiñones-Ortiz, has checked a number of references and helped with the bibliography. And my wife, Catherine, who is Professor of Church History at Columbia Theological Seminary, has read the manuscript and, as always, made helpful and perceptive observations.

Such debts I certainly cannot repay. I simply pray that the use I have made of these various contributions will be of value in our present Fuenteovejuna.

FOREWORD

Justo González and I have been good friends for many years. I suspect that our friendship, our Christian faith, and our common cause provide a good example of the new ecumenism Justo speaks about in this fascinating work, which constantly intertwines the contemporary Hispanic struggle with the Christian tradition. I know of no other person who could have accomplished such an intriguing and provoking work, for Justo González is at one and the same time a top-notch scholar among scholars and a full-blooded Hispanic among Hispanics. He inserts the Hispanic struggle within the 2000 years of Christianity and interprets the deviations, corrections, councils, ecumenical definitions, dogmas, and doctrines in light of the Hispanic struggle, and vice versa. Truly this is a much-needed and remarkable work.

I suspect Justo and I became good friends from the very beginning because we are at one and the same time so similar and so different. We are both Hispanics of the Christian tradition living in the United States. Justo is Cuban born, while I am *Tejano* and U.S. born. In high school, he was the Protestant among Catholics while I was the *Mexicano* Catholic among Anglo Protestants. He had the experience of going into exile, while I lived the experience of being a foreigner in my own native land of birth. Justo is a scholar who is very concerned with things pastoral, while I am a pastor who is very concerned with scholarship in the service of ministry. As a Protestant in Cuba, Justo was a strange minority within a Catholic people; as a Mexican Catholic in the United States, I had the experience of being an ignored and often despised minority within an Irish-German U.S. Catholic Church and within the greater Protestant culture of the United States.

Justo is very secure in his Methodist denomination and thus very at ease with other Protestants and with Catholics, while I am very secure in my own Roman Catholic Church and thus very at ease with Protestants. In fact, one could easily say that Justo is a Catholic Protestant while Virgilio is a Protestant Catholic. Justo is no less Protestant because of his acceptance and love of our Hispanic cultural catholicity, while I do not feel any less Catholic because I have accepted and love many of the aspects of Protestantism that have enriched my life and my faith. Neither one of us is interested in converting the other or in proving the other wrong. I suspect both of us enjoy our Catholic-Protestant *mestizaje*, which might appear strange to others but is so enriching for us that we hope to bring others into this new expression of Hispanic Christianity.

Our friendship clicked from the very beginning because we both shared our one Christian faith, our common Iberoamerican heritage, our language, our experience of segregation, our love for our people, and our commitment to the struggles for justice of the poor, the oppressed, the enslaved, the marginal, the exploited, the silenced, the unemployed, the undocumented, the abused, the underpaid, the unprotected. We have both seen the suffering faces of our people, we have heard the cries of those "justly" but immorally condemned to prisons, we have agonized with the refugees who are apprehended and deported as if they were common criminals, we have lived the frustration of the growing number of Hispanic school dropouts, the emptiness of those enslaved by drugs, the painfulness of those increasing numbers who are dying of AIDS.

Yes, we shared the scandal, the outrage, and the anger at our respective churches, which are often concerned with great buildings, well-planned worship services, orthodox theologies, and appropriate liturgical songs but have no knowledge of the suffering of the millions of Lazaruses all around them. We shared the frustration with schools of theology and theologies, whether liberal or conservative, Protestant or Catholic, fundamentalist or mainline, who ignore the needs of the poor and dispossessed of this world and continue to read Scripture and the Christian tradition from within the perspective of the rich, the nicely installed, and the powerful of this world. Theologies, churches, and preaching seem more concerned with helping people feel good about being in this world with all its hedonistic tendencies than with calling individuals and nations to a true conversion to the way of Jesus of Nazareth. There seemed to be much more concern with the Christ of Glory who could justify the glories of our United States way of life than with Jesus of Nazareth who lived and died as a scandal to all the respectable, religious, and fine people of *this world*! The churches have often presented the Glory of Christ more in terms of the glories and

10

glitter of this sinful world, thus preventing the true light of the Glory of Christ from illuminating the darkness of our present society.

Justo and I share the suffering of our people, but we also share the deep faith of our people in the whole mystery of Christ: the incarnation, the cross, the resurrection, and Pentecost! He truly became one of us that we might have new life! He became a curse and a scandal for us so that we who are considered to be the curse and scandal of this world might become the source of blessing and salvation for our world. He became the reject of the world so that in and through him the rejects of today's world might appear as what they really are: God's chosen and anointed ones.

When God became man, he did not become just any man. He became a Galilean Jew, Son of Mary—he became a despised person of a despised people, a man whose earthly father was unknown. He truly became human rubbish for our salvation. The ways of God are truly incomprehensible—especially to the important, dignified, well-qualified and well-placed, honorable, and important people of society. No wonder that the well-installed like to speak about the triumphant Christ, while the poor and the lowly prefer to speak about suffering, flagellated, and crowned with thorns Jesus of Nazareth! One justifies power and glory while the other assures us that the God of life is with us in suffering and struggles. But neither one is complete without the other. Jesus is not complete without Christ for Jesus is the Christ, but Christ cannot be known or appreciated if we do not "go to Galilee that you might see him" (Mark 16:7; Matt. 28:7, 10).

To confess Christ without knowing Jesus is to create an idol for ourselves who will more cover the face, the mind, and the heart of God than reveal them. Too often people confess Christ the Lord as the embodiment of all the good things of this world: success, power, prestige, material security, good vacations, elegant clothes, jewels, fancy cars, and the like. The good things of this world replace Jesus as the Christ. No wonder that this type of Christianity, which has nothing to do with the way of Jesus of Nazareth, is so appealing to the masses of this world. Is this not the Christ that is frequently preached in U.S. fundamentalism and mainline churches? In many of our churches there is often more a call to feel good than a call to discipleship. Those who are committing themselves to the service of the poor in Latin American, in the Philippines, and in other poor areas of the world certainly are answering the call to discipleship. But this call to Christian discipleship seems to be more and more rare in the churches of the Western world.

The civil justice of his day condemned Jesus as a common criminal, but God raised him to be our Christ. The powerful of his time appeared

11

to have triumphed when they had him arrested and killed, yet they could not destroy him because the power of the God of life was within him. Just when they thought he was finished, he had just begun. They tried to get rid of one man but soon afterward there were twelve, and within the blinking of an eye, the new way of the carpenter of Nazareth was captivating not only the poor, the orphans, the servants, the slaves, and the outcasts, but equally the priests, the military leaders, the intellectuals, and those in government. Those that knew what life was all about had asked, "What good can come out of Galilee?" and to their amazement, the greatest hope of a truly new life started with the crucified Galilean who in his lifetime had been a friend of scoundrels and public sinners! God has such a magnificent sense of humor, and it is thanks to that sense of humor that the crying of today's world can enjoy such healthy laughter while the seemingly joyful who are surrounded with privilege and pleasure are often rotting from within with sadness and emptiness, nicely camouflaged by the many layers of makeup, designer clothes, and endless parties. Yes, because of God's incredible sense of humor, today's poor and suffering can sing and dance and shout for joy because we know God's secret! We know that our liberation is at hand and that in and through our struggles, the reign of God is at hand.

Yes, we know that the day will come (in fact, in many ways it is already here) when there will be no more borders in the Americas and people will freely travel back and forth at will, there will be no more dictators or fake-democracies but all will live together as one family, the former military generals will be managers of large farms while the former navy admirals will head fishing fleets so that by their common work, there will be no more poor or hungry—how beautiful it will be to convert them from agents of death into agents of life. Yes, I see the day when there will be no more border patrols and the former agents of the *migra* will assist the new immigrant in finding housing and employment. Yes, the day will come when the rich will go to eat *frijoles y tacos* with the poor while inviting them to their homes to enjoy their swimming pools, beautiful gardens, and plentiful barbecues. I see the day coming when the rich will convert and discover that their own wealth is the root source of their increasing unhappiness and thus freely choose to share their wealth with others. In so doing they will discover a happiness and a fulfillment they never dreamed possible. The poor too will convert and discover their innermost dignity and call. They too will come forth from the tombs of silence and powerlessness to be a voice and a power in the buildup of a new culture and a new civilization.

Yes, there is truly a new ecumenism in the common struggle for justice, but there is also a new ecumenism in the new knowledge that is emerging out of the common struggle. It is just beginning. It is not yet developed. Justo has pointed to two of the elements: our common struggle for justice and the Catholic discovery of the Bible. This is certainly a good common ground to begin our common task of the development of a new theological knowledge. But I would dare to suggest a third element that I think will be essential. Hispanic Catholics have discovered the Bible and are fascinated with it, and Protestants are very happy with this development. But for the most part Hispanic Protestants have not yet discovered and reclaimed as their own the marvelous aspects of our Iberoamerican Catholic heritage that they left behind in becoming Protestants. It is precisely this aspect that I admire so much about Justo! He is so comfortable celebrating our common Iberoamerican religious heritage.

Let us never forget that we Iberoamericanos are not descendants of the religious and cultural problems of Europe, which produced Protestantism and post-Tridentine Catholicism. We are descendants of neither, and therefore should never be forced to assume them in order to be called Christians. We are descendants of two great mystical traditions: the pre-Reformation evangelically renewed Iberian and the Native American. Both were quite different from Reformation and Counter-Reformation European Christianity! The evangelical humanism of Erasmus and Cardinal Cisneros mingled with the mystical religions of the peoples of these lands to give birth to our *Mestizo* Iberoamerican Christianity. This providential synthesis is at the very roots of our birth as the *Mestizo* people of the Americas. Into the United States came the children of the Reformation, Protestants and Counter-Reformation Catholics, while in Latin America a totally new expression of Christianity was in the process of being born, one that had nothing to do with either the Reformation or the Counter-Reformation. Today, this new church of Latin America, which was born at the very beginning of the Americas, is being threatened by very sincere but narrow-minded (Anglo-centric) Catholics and Protestants who do not understand or appreciate the identity of the new church. This church has developed not according to the Protestant or Catholic molds of Europe or the United States, but in accordance with the inner dynamics of the Spirit, which is actively at work among the entire people of God who share in the Iberoamerican heritage.

We are *Mestizo* Christians, and this *mestizo* tradition can enrich the Protestant and Catholic traditions of the United States. Furthermore, because it is the Christian religious expression of the millions of poor, oppressed, and marginated peoples of the Americas, it has within it the potential of redeeming the Christian religious expression of Europe and the United States. It is the Christian poor of today's world that will bring salvation to the Christians of the rich nations of the world, who because of the material wealth of their own nations are too blind to see the truth of the gospel. How often we hear missionaries who thought they were going to save the Latin American poor come back to confess that it was they who experienced redemption; that rather than preaching the gospel, it was they who truly heard the gospel in its radical beauty and simplicity for the first time.

The failure to recognize the birth and existence of this new *Mestizo* Christianity, which is both in communion with the universal church and its traditions and has an identity and faith expressions peculiar to (its) own historical-cultural uniqueness, has brought about disastrous consequences. It seems to me that quite often the deepest treasures of our Catholic-Iberoamerican culture were too easily identified with the dogmas, rites, and rituals of the Roman Catholic Church. Likewise, the Bible has been read and interpreted by the Protestants through the eyes of the Nordic European culture that produced Protestantism. Thus Latin Americans have been asked to abandon their common roots and become Nordic Europeans in the name of the gospel! Quite often, conversion to Protestantism (from Roman Catholicism) seemed to demand an uprooting of the religious-cultural ethos that formed the deepest roots of our Hispanic culture and collective identity. It is for this reason that I object to Protestantism and even more so to fundamentalism. In the name of the God of life, they destroy the collective soul of our people. I believe that one can convert to Christ without abandoning one's religious-cultural identity. I am a Hispanic Catholic who is each day seeking to continue my conversion to Christ and his ways. I think I know the Scriptures quite well, and there is nothing in my Iberoamerican Catholic culture that I feel I have to reject in order to be a good Christian. As we know the full mystery of Jesus of Nazareth more and more, there will certainly be an on-going reinterpretation and transformation of our deepest religious symbols, but there does not have to be an elimination of them. Christianity does not come to destroy but to bring to the fullness of life!

Let me illustrate what I am trying to say. When an Anglo-American changes from one confessional affiliation to another, there is no great traumatic break in family ties. Changing churches is part of U.S. culture! No great thing. Within Anglo-American culture, one "converts" from one Christian denomination to another, or even from the Christian religion to another religion, within the same culture and hence without any great fuss. You don't have to abandon U.S. culture in order to change to another religion. This is not so amongst Hispanics.

14

Often the change from Catholicism to another denomination totally fragments the family and the relatives. It is a traumatic break that brings about much suffering to all the parties involved. In the former case (United States), one changes religions without abandoning one's cultural heritage, while in the latter case, conversion demands a total break with one's culture. In the former, one continues to be a member of one's people, while in the latter, one has to abandon and betray one's people to convert to the religion and the culture of the other!

But the Protestants have not been the only ones demanding an uprooting. Too many post-Vatican II Catholics have equally demanded the conversion from one cultural expression of Catholicism to another in the name of the gospel. Pastoral agents of mainline United States Catholicism have not understood or appreciated our Latin American expression of the gospel as it has been transmitted though various generations, and have demanded that we abandon our *sensus fidelium* in order to become "good Catholics." The quasi-monastic mold of post-Vatican II Catholicism seeks to make mini-monks or junior clerics of all the laity, while the Iberoamerican religious expressions of the masses invite the clergy and the religious to become an integral part of the celebrations of the people of God.

Monasticism or clericalism have never been a part of the religious heritage of the practices and traditions of the people. On the other hand, processions, pilgrims, *fiestas patronales, altarcitos caseros, posadas, pastorelas, acostada y leventada del niño, Reyes, crucifixión y santo entierro*, and many other popular celebrations that did not depend on the presence of the clergy have been the deepest and most meaningful elements of our Iberoamerican religious tradition. The clergy have done their thing in the sanctuary, while the people of God have celebrated their faith in the homes, in the streets, and in the main plazas of their towns. Since the masses of our people were never allowed into the ranks of the clergy or religious, their clerical celebrations seemed more like the distant rites of foreigners than intimate celebrations of the faithful. It is quite notable that the chief religious celebrations of our people are nowhere to be found in the official rituals of the Roman Catholic Church. They are truly the faith celebrations of the people of God in which the bishops, clergy, and religious are most welcome, but not missed if they are not around.

The Christian expressions of our ancestors were no more perfect than any European or USA expression of Christianity, but neither were they inferior, false, or, worse yet, pagan. They were, like any other expression of Christianity, authentic while being limited and in need of improvement. Every cultural expression of Christianity has to be in a constant process of purification in relation to the gospel, otherwise it transforms its every expressions of the gospel into idols and imposes them upon other peoples as absolutes. This type of idolatry of one's own ways has dominated many generations of European and U.S. missionary activity and continues to do so today. It is through these idolatrous attitudes and practices that fundamentalists, Protestants, and mainline U.S. Catholics have attempted to destroy the cultural-religious ethos of the Hispanic peoples. They have been quick (and often mistaken) in pointing out our idols, while remaining totally blind to the idols within the United States (Protestant, fundamentalist, or Catholic) religious-cultural heritage. U.S. religions are quick to point out the defects of the religions of other peoples but remain totally blind to the idols they accept and venerate, without even recognizing them as such within the mainline culture of the United States. And often, it is (with) these very idols of the United States that they want to replace our Iberoamerican imagery of the living God. In the name of God they want us to replace God with mammon!

For a suffering and oppressed people, there is nothing more powerful than one's collective religious symbols. They are the roots of our existence and the source of our identity. They put us in contact with our ancestors and guarantee our life to future generations. They are the language of resistance and protest. In them and through them, no one of us is alone, for we are all in one and one in all. In them we are who we are *y no le pedimos nada a nadie!* They need no explanation to us, but they will never make sense to the outsider. They are no more or no less than the living mystery of our collective existence. Take them away from us, and we cease to exist as a people. Help us to celebrate them, and you bring us the good news of life. They are not problems to be solved or superstitions to be eliminated but the deep symbols of faith of *this* particular people of God on pilgrimage to the promised land. They are the roots of our life as a people, and without them we will cease to exist as a people.

Whether walking together the Way of the Cross on Good Friday, or walking with Caesar Chavez behind the banner of *Nuestra Señora de Guadalupe*, or singing the *mazes* during our sunrise service on the feast of *Nuestra Señora de Guadalupe*, or making a pilgrimage together to *Nuestra Señora de Los Lagos*, or visiting the cemetery on the *día de los muertos* (All Hallows' Eve), or singing the *Alabados* that were taught to us by our grandmothers we had the consciousness that we were a people united and strong. Others may look down upon us, but our *madrecita* calls us forth to be her trusted messengers.

16

Let me be very clear—I do not want to say that every Hispanic has to remain a member of the Roman Catholic Church in order to be a Hispanic, but I am saying that when a Hispanic ceases to be catholic (to participate in the religious-cultural expressions of our people), he or she ceases to be a Hispanic. But it should be equally clear that the most cherished religious-cultural expressions of the people are certainly practiced in some Roman Catholic Churches while despised in others, yet they are not the sole property of the Roman Catholic Church. They do not appear in the official rituals of Roman Catholics, and one could certainly be a good Roman Catholic without accepting or practicing the favorite religious expressions of the people. I have no doubt some will disagree. This is my own conviction, which becomes stronger and stronger.

I am not against Hispanics practicing their Christian faith in churches other than my own cherished Roman Catholic Church. It certainly hurts me to see them leave for another home, but I have to admit that if parents cannot feed their children, it is good for the children to go to the neighbor's home for nourishment, and many of our people who were not receiving proper nourishment in our Catholic churches are going to other churches to satisfy their spiritual hunger. Some Hispanic Catholics have been chased away from the Catholic Church by insensitive and ignorant Catholic pastors. Yet it really hurts when the one feeding the children takes advantage of the needy children to destroy the very identity and name of the very children they are nourishing. Our Christianity as expressed through the blend of our Iberian and Native American heritage is our identity and name. We can go to any church we choose to go to, but we should not be asked to change our name and destroy our identity in order to be accepted. Being reborn in Christ certainly transforms us from within, but it does not destroy us. We do not cease being Black, Chicano, Cuban-exile, or Puerto Rican, nor do we cease liking *tamales* or *pastelitos, cumbias* or *polkitas*, nor do we forget our history or the road we have traveled, or give up the treasures of our heritage. Our religious heritage is our collective soul and spirit. We want to be saved, but we do not want to be destroyed in the name of Christ! We want to be saved not just as individuals but as a people, and as a people we cannot be saved if our innermost soul is destroyed!

It is through our ancestors that we have received our Holy Faith. It is for us, in fidelity to them and to the God of our life, to assume their sacred ways and, in dialogue with the Scriptures, perfect and ennoble them, but never ridicule, destroy, or abandon them. Our ancestors survived many hardships and endured many pains. Our tradition has been one of suffering and insult. Thanks to their power to endure, you

17

and I are here today. Where did they get the force to endure their death-bearing existence if it was not from their unquestioned faith in the incomprehensible wisdom of the God who saves us? In our suffering we were never alone because our Jesus on the cross was suffering with us. He was the guarantee that God had not abandoned us, and our *madrecita santísima* was always there, protecting us, listening to us, encouraging us. When there was no one around to listen to our cries, she was always there. When others tried to scatter us, she was around to bring us together in her bosom. When there were no clergy to minister to us, our grandmothers were around to bless us, to pray for us, and to offer a *velita* (candle) as the sacrifice of the poor. Our faith was not false! It was simple and profound. It was not cerebral, doctrinal, or clerical. It resided in our hearts. Our faith was so deep that we did not hesitate to give our life for its defense, as was evident during the Cristero Wars in Mexico. Our Christian faith was our life, and without it there was no life.

I find it insulting and disgusting when anyone—Catholic, Protestant, or fundamentalist—dares to ridicule or insult the faith of our ancestors. They lived and died for our Christian faith. We have martyrs, mystics, and saints. I am grateful to God that I am a descendant of this rich tradition of faith, and I feel sorry for those of our own who do not know it or appreciate it. An even worse insult is for officials of our own Roman Catholic Church to fail to appreciate or promote the religious expression of our Iberoamerican tradition.

There is yet another reason why I feel so strongly about our Iberoamerican religious heritage. There is no doubt that the Scriptures present us a God who is prejudiced in favor of the poor, the suffering, and the outcasts of the world. If the poor are God's privileged, then I contend that the God imagery of the poor is the privileged imagery of God. Their expressions of God are much more accurate and closer to the truth about God than the best theologies about God, formulated by persons who are removed from the everyday struggles of God's chosen "little ones" of this world. "Father, Lord of heaven and earth, to you I offer praise; for what you have hidden from the learned and the clever you have revealed to the merest children. Father, it is true. You have graciously willed it so" (Matt. 11:25–26). The masses of our people are the poor and the destitute of this world. They are the privileged biblical "little ones" of today's church and world. To them, God is especially present in a very intimate and personal way.

If I had a true-or-false test to answer and were given the choice between the biblical and theological interpretations that emerge out of the Christians of the rich and installed nations of the world and the interpretations that emerge spontaneously out of the suffering people of the poor nations of the world, I would have no doubt as to which one was the correct answer. The poor have a privileged knowledge of God and of the language of God, for they are God's chosen ones, and God communicates with them in the language that is natural to them.

I am the pastor of a very large parish of the poorest of San Antonio, Texas. Each day I discover new and fascinating aspects about God in the faith expressions of my people. And as I reflect upon my own faith journey and recall the faith of my grandparents and my parents, I recognize that I learned much more about the God of our Christian faith from them than I have from the finest theologians of our Catholic or Protestant churches. Our theologians speak a lot about God, but my parents and grandparents knew God personally. Their knowledge of God continues to be much more dynamic and exciting, for it is far better to know someone personally than merely to know a lot about someone. My family never read the Scriptures and knew nothing about the formal teachings of our Catholic Church, but they were people of deep faith and fascinating theological insights. My father hardly knew how to read, but his understanding of God is still my own most precious under-standing of God today—far richer than any I have encountered in the best of theologians I have read or studied. Our people were not people of books, but they were definitely people of a profound and living faith. Faith for them was not a theological ideology or a bunch of theological propositions to be believed, denied, or argued, or even an endless litany of biblical quotes. Faith was the unquestioned personal knowledge, trust, and love of the God who is the source of our existence—*en la divina providencia*.

Yes, a new ecumenism is in the making, which is far beyond the ecumenical efforts of the Western world. Our ecumenical enterprise in the Iberoamerican New World will surprise everyone! We will transcend the problems of the Old World, which were imposed upon us by foreigners who did not understand us, and in so doing will offer new insights into the Christian mystery that the Western world has not imagined or suspected. Yes, a new church is in the making, which will be ever more universal—not by making everyone carbon copies, but by being large enough to accept everyone in their differences. We will no longer impoverish our understanding of God by limiting God to the ways of knowledge of the Western World; we will come to the knowledge of a far greater God by knowing God also through the categories of thought of our own *mestizo* world of Iberoamerica. We can all enrich one another, but no one of us should seek to destroy or compete with the others.

Justo opens the way for this new religious *mestizaje*, a new and fruitful encounter of traditions, which will be the Christian expression of the future. What today appears to be opposing and contradictory ways will tomorrow be appreciated as elements of the new religious expression. It will be like a new Pentecost, and in Christ we will all be a new creation—*el Cristianismo mestizo de las Américas*! The truth of the gospel will be known and appreciated not only in the mind but even more so in the heart, which is concerned with ultimate reality in terms of *flor y canto*. We will worship not only in word and song but in dance and collective ritual. We will work not only for the salvation of individuals but for the salvation of peoples. The gospel of Our Lord Jesus Christ will certainly enrich the life and cultures of the Americas as our own Iberoamerican heritage brings out new aspects of the gospel that have heretofore been unsuspected.

A new day is beginning, and it is great to be a part of it!

Virgilio P. Elizondo
Fiesta de Nuestra Señora de Guadalupe
Diciembre 12, 1989

CHAPTER 1

The Significance
of a Minority Perspective

What follows is not an unbiased theological treatise. It does not even seek to be unbiased. On the contrary, the author is convinced that every theological perspective, no matter how seemingly objective, betrays a bias of which the theologian is not usually aware. Obviously, some theologies are more biased than others. But before we attempt to pass such judgments, we must be aware of the bias that is inherent in the judgment itself. Deep-sea divers tell us that in an ocean environment, where everything is moving, what most draws their attention is not what moves, as happens on land, but rather what stands still. Likewise, when it comes to detecting prejudice or even tendentiousness in a theology, we must not be too quick to pass judgment on those views that differ from the established norm. It may well be that our common views, precisely because they are common, involve a prejudice that is difficult for us to see, and that a seemingly more biased view will help us discover that prejudice. This is probably one of the most significant contributions that a minority perspective can make to the church at large.

This does not mean, however, that the task of theology will then be to bring together all these various perspectives, compare them, and seek to produce a theology that is free from every bias. This has been the manner in which many in the academic world have approached the theological enterprise. There is a great deal to be said for the academic goal of rational objectivity. But if there is one thing that can be said with absolute certainty about the God of Scripture, it is that God cannot be known through rational objectivity.

Furthermore, one could even go so far as to say that the God of Scripture is not an unbiased God. God has certain purposes for creation and is moving the world and humankind toward the fulfillment of those purposes. This means that, in a sense, God is biased against anything

21

that stands in the way of those goals, and in favor of all that aids them. If this is true, the task of theology will not be to produce some sort of neutral—and therefore inane—interpretation of the nature of God and the universe, but rather to discover the purposes of God, to read the "signs of the times," and to call the church to obedience in the present situation.

This in turn means that theology cannot be done in the abstract. There is no such thing as a "general" theology. There is indeed a Christian community that is held together by bonds of a common faith. But within that community we each bring our own history and perspective to bear on the message of the gospel, hoping to help the entire community to discover dimensions that have gone unseen and expecting to be corrected when necessary.

Given this situation, a brief statement regarding the author's perspective seems to be in order.

The Experience of Being a Member of a Religious Minority

I grew up in Latin America, in a country where hardly 4 or 5 percent of the population was Protestant. It was also a time and a place where Protestantism was understood almost exclusively in terms of opposition to everything Catholic, and where most Catholics knew very little about Protestants, beyond the fact that we were heretics. Most of my classmates in high school were Catholic in a very superficial manner. But some others were very devout, and one of the manifestations of their devotion was that they crossed themselves when they learned that I was a Protestant. There were long and passionate debates—whispered in the library and shouted in the playing field—about the authority of the pope, the need for confession, the mediating role of the saints, the authority of Scripture, and a dozen subjects about which neither of the parties involved knew a great deal.

As I now look back upon those experiences, I realize that they influenced my theological outlook on several points.

The most important of these—and one to which I still hold—is the authority of Scripture. When one is a member of a minority, and the entire establishment is trying to convince one that one is wrong, it is necessary, for sheer psychological and political survival, to find an authority that goes beyond the hostile environment. This my friends and I found in Scripture, which had the added advantage that it was an authority that our opponents acknowledged. To argue on the basis of consensus or even common sense was futile, for we soon learned that "common" sense is indeed the sense of the community, and that there was little we could gain on the basis of it. But if I could prove to my classmates that the Bible was on my side on some particular issue, soon I would have them confounded and running to their priests for answers to my arguments. Later experiences of theological education and reflection have affected my understanding of the authority and the message of Scripture. But to this day I have never been tempted by a shallow liberalism that equates the biblical message with the supposedly "best" features of our society. There are many theological reasons why I have felt compelled to reject that facile approach. But I suspect that behind those theological reasons still stand the earlier experiences of my naive debates with my classmates.

Another point at which the experience of being a member of a religious minority influenced my outlook was my view of world history. In search of vindication outside our immediate environment, we often turned toward the United States and Protestant Europe. In many ways, both spoken and implicit, my fellow believers and I came to the conclusion that North American culture was more Christian, and more advanced, than ours. Missionaries have often been blamed for spreading such views. There is no doubt that many of them had difficulty distinguishing between the gospel and North American culture. But as I now look back upon those days, I must confess that there were many reasons why we ourselves were ready to accept such a confusion of Christianity and culture. In the midst of a society built on the general assumption of an agreement between Catholicism and culture, we found it comforting to be able to point to another society where there seemed to be a similar connection between Protestantism and culture. And we found it particularly comforting when we could point to the technological, political, and economic triumphs of that society. Later events have radically altered my views on this matter. But such views were a significant part of the experience of being a member of a religious minority.

Furthermore, this was—and still is—a widespread view among Protestants in Latin America. Out of a sense of gratitude and loyalty to the early missionaries, and to the millions in the United States who still support their churches, many Latin American Protestants feel that they owe a measure of loyalty to the United States and to its culture. Such feelings are part of the motivation of many Protestant Latin Americans who migrate to the United States, and therefore in Hispanic Protestantism in the United States there is a core group of those who believe that any criticism of the society in which they now live is disloyal, not only to their adopted nation but also to their religion. Although many who come to this country with such views soon change them as a result of the oppressive and racist situations in which they find themselves, their place is taken by new Protestant immigrants, and therefore there is always in Hispanic-American Protestantism a significant number of those who hold the same views of North American culture and society that I held in my earlier days. One of the urgent pastoral tasks in Hispanic Protestantism is to help these people in their pilgrimage, showing them that Scripture gives them leave to be themselves.

Finally, a third way in which those early experiences colored my theological outlook was my view of the relationship between the church and the world. For us, the church was very much a refuge from a hostile world. We had an overpowering sense of mission. But this had very little to do with changing the world around us and was centered on the goal of adding other refugees to our Christian community. Further study of Scripture has long since taken me beyond that point. But I still feel a deep kinship for the early Anabaptist view of the church as distinct from the civil community, and never coextensive with it. In my youth, I was constantly placed before a difficult choice: I decided either for the life and values of the Christian community or for those of the society around me. There was no third alternative. Today, I still find it difficult to belong to a church where such radical demands are seldom made. Although I no longer agree with Kierkegaard's existentialism, nor with his stance as the lone knight of faith, I still resound to his poignant criticism of a Christendom in which faith has become the mainstay of middle-class decency:

> In the magnificent cathedral the Honorable and Right Reverend Geheime-General-Ober-Hof-Pradikant, the elect favorite of the fashionable world, appears before an elect company and preaches with emotion upon the text he himself elected: "God hath elected the base things of the world, and the things that are despised"—and nobody laughs.[1]

The type of Christianity that was common among the majority of the population in the United States went to my homeland and taught me how to be part of a Christian minority. And now that various circumstances have brought me to the land whence the missionaries came, I find that the minority stance that they taught me forces me to rebel against the Christianity that sent them!

The Experience of Being a Member of an Ethnic Minority

At a later stage in my life, the experience of being a member of a minority took on a different dimension. This was when I came to live in the United States and found that although now my religion was that of the majority, I had now become part of an ethnic minority. This awareness came to me by stages, and I still remember minor incidents that prompted me along the way. Some of these incidents would seem to be a case of hypersensitivity to any who have not experienced them. I remember, for instance, arriving at a store in New Haven, Connecticut, and having two clerks follow me, as if they expected me to steal something. And I remember my first faculty meeting in a white teaching institution many years later, when a suggestion I had made was completely ignored until, later in the discussion, it was made by a white colleague, at which time it was enthusiastically received. But these personal incidents played only a minor role, for what they did was to give me the freedom to look at North American society with a critical eye and to see what was being done not only to Hispanics, but also to Afro-Americans, to farm laborers of whatever race, and to Native Americans. At a later time, this rising consciousness came to include women, the elderly, and others. Thus my experience of being a minority in the ethnic sense opened my eyes and ears to the oppression that is very much a part of our society, and to hear the voice of the oppressed who are crying out, often in the name of Christianity.

The result of all this for me is that the authority of Scripture has been heightened, but its thrust has been somewhat changed. I still believe that it is the authority of Scripture that can provide us with a needed corrective that comes from beyond the mores and prejudices of society. In this country, as in Latin America, this appeal to Scripture has the added advantage that many in the ruling group claim to acknowledge biblical authority. Thus if we can show that the witness of Scripture is on our side in our present struggles, this will provide us with significant leverage against all sorts of oppression.

But there is more to the question of the authority of Scripture. It is a well-known fact that the Bible has been used repeatedly in order to support repression and injustice. In Latin America, the Spanish conquest was justified on the basis of supposedly biblical teaching. In both North and South America, the Bible has been used to destroy significant cultures and civilizations. Again, in both continents Paul's authority has been adduced in favor of slavery. In the United States, even after the abolition of slavery, and to this day, white supremacists claim that the Bible is on their side. Those—both men and women—who wish to keep

25

women subservient are constantly quoting the Pauline and Deutero-Pauline Epistles.

Under such circumstances, it is not surprising that many among the groups in this country who feel oppressed are inclined to abandon any attempt to accept or claim the biblical faith. A growing number of women born within the church are convinced that the Bible is essentially a sexist book and therefore have dissociated themselves from it.[2] Some Native Americans, in their quest for roots and a sense of identity, are exalting the religion of their ancestors and claiming that Christianity is pale-face religion.[3] A similar movement has existed among Afro-Americans for decades,[4] as can be seen in the appeal of the Black Muslims.[5] Among Hispanics, there is a growing tendency toward radical secularization and bitterness. This secularization, however, is not due to the intellectual difficulties with which academic theologians often deal but rather to the existential difficulty that the gospel of love is not translated into actual good news.

At the same time, precisely among these oppressed groups, there is a strong movement of return to "the old time religion," with its promise of heavenly rewards and its acceptance of the earthly status quo. Among Afro-Americans, Hispanics, Native Americans, and poor whites, this phenomenon is quite noticeable in the growth of the fundamentalist churches, which, as will become apparent in the pages that follow, are not much closer to the fundamentals of biblical faith than are the liberals. Among certain groups of women, a parallel phenomenon can be seen in the present popularity of books and movements that promise marital bliss in exchange for submission, supposedly on the basis of biblical authority.[6]

But these are not the only options open to us. Among women and the various ethnic minorities, there are also an increasingly significant number of people who believe that when one reads Scripture correctly, one comes out with different conclusions—conclusions that are both liberating and true to the biblical message.[7]

In summary—and in ways that will become clearer in the chapters that follow—the experience of being part of an ethnic minority has led me to reinterpret the meaning of the Bible, which I still cherish as a result of my previous experience of being part of a religious minority.

The Changing Latin American Scene

A great deal has changed in Latin America since the days when I debated religion with my classmates. This is not the place to describe all those changes. But it is necessary to acknowledge one particular, significant change that has taken place in Latin America, and that has helped shape a great deal of what I shall have to say in my later chapters.

In recent years, the Roman Catholic Church in Latin America has taken increasing cognizance of its responsibility toward the impoverished masses of the continent.[8] This responsibility includes the preaching of the gospel and the administration of the sacraments—and there are many priests whose ministry is limited to that. But it includes also genuine care for the physical and psychological needs of those masses. At first, the leaders in this movement were concerned almost exclusively with the immediate needs of individuals and small communities. But they soon came to the conclusion that they were struggling against conditions that were derived from the very structure of society, and that the demand of the gospel was therefore that they address themselves not only to the immediate needs of their parishioners but also to the task of creating a more just society. Since the Roman Catholic Church is quite powerful in many Latin American countries—or at least seems to be so—this newly discovered responsibility has led to many confrontations with repressive governments in various countries. The leaders of the movement are convinced that their struggle is not only against such repressive governments but also against the national and international economic structures that support them.[9] The result is that dozens of priests—and an archbishop—have died under mysterious circumstances, while the number of lay leaders—both men and women—who have suffered a similar fate is beyond counting. A list only of those who have died in the relatively small country of Guatemala, for instance, reads like the worst reports of persecution in pre-Constantinian times. All this has led many in the Roman Catholic Church in Latin America to a reassessment of its tradition, which in many points is quite similar to the reinterpretation of Scripture that I propose here. This reassessment has been linked to a return to scriptural authority, and thus a new form of ecumenism has developed that would have astounded the great proponents of ecumenism of a few decades ago.

The other side of this ecumenism is the changes that have taken place within Protestantism. The Protestantism that I knew in my youth, with its strong anti-Catholic emphasis and its pro-American sentiment, still exists. But alongside it there is a new Protestantism, one that has matured and has begun to interpret Scripture and theology in its own way. Much of this has taken place through the influence of developments within Catholicism, but much of it is also the result of the reflection of Protestants as they become more deeply rooted in their cultures and in the social and economic struggles of their nations.[10] This new Protestantism is more ready to enter into genuine dialogue and collaboration with the new Catholicism.[11]

Thus Protestants and Catholics are working together toward a more just society. But they are not doing this simply on the basis of the traditional Catholic and Protestant theologies. Rather, they are rediscovering forgotten aspects of their traditions and their sources of authority and finding that on the basis of these new discoveries they are often called to a common task in the world. Or, in other terms, one could say that what has happened is that, by virtue of their social stance, the more radical leaders of the Roman Catholic Church have found themselves attacked by those in power—including many in the hierarchy—[12] and have thus had to appeal to the biblical bases for their actions, much as I found myself having recourse to the Bible in my earlier debates with my classmates.

This brief discussion of recent events in Latin America is important to our task because in many ways those events influence the lives of Hispanics in this country. To this we shall return in a later chapter, for events in Latin America greatly affect the Hispanic community in the United States. But rather than dealing with the more distant Latin American situation, the purpose of this essay is to deal first of all with the situation in which we ourselves live: the United States.

Fuenteovejuna Theology

Lope de Vega's play, *Fuenteovejuna*, tells the story of the small town of that name, which was under the tyrannical rule of Don Fernán Gómez, knight commander of the Order of Calatrava. After much suffering, the townspeople finally rebel and kill the commander, placing his head on a pike as the banner of their freedom. Their battle cry is "Fuenteovejuna, *todos a una*" (Fuenteovejuna, all are one). When the Grand Master of the Order hears of this, he appeals to Ferdinand and Isabella, who appoint a judge-inquisitor to find the guilty parties and punish them. The judge, however, finds that he can make little progress in his inquiry, for whenever he asks, "*¿Quién mató al comendador?*" (Who killed the commander?), the answer is always the same: "Fuenteovejuna, señor" (Fuenteovejuna, my lord). Irritated, he puts three hundred of the local inhabitants to torture. Still, from all of them—men, women, children, people in their old age—the answer is the same: "Fuenteovejuna, señor." Finally the judge asks for instructions from Isabella and Ferdinand, who respond that, given such unanimity, there must have been just cause for the commander's death.

The interesting point, however, is that when the townspeople respond "Fuenteovejuna, señor," they are not simply trying to cover up for one another. What has happened is that through their suffering and final uprising, such solidarity has arisen that they do believe that it was the town, and not any individuals in it, that killed the commander. Not only will they not fix individual responsibility; they could not do so even if they tried. "Fuenteovejuna, *todos a una*," has become more than a battle cry and is now the very reality by which they live.[13]

This book is very much like Fuenteovejuna. It includes material and insights gleaned from hundreds of encounters and discussions with Hispanics in all walks of life and with various levels of theological sophistication. I remember some insights that came to me in Sunday school in a Pentecostal church in the Bronx. I remember others that came from students many years ago at the Seminario Evangélico de Puerto Rico. Also, much of the material included here has been the subject of discussion of a group of friends who, under the title of "Hispanic Instructors," have been meeting regularly at Perkins School of Theology for several years. The dialogue has certainly included books and articles by colleagues from all over the world. But by and large, I would be hard pressed to determine where or from whom I gained a particular insight. All I can say is that what appears in the pages that follow expresses much of what I have shared with and learned from my Hispanic sisters and brothers over the course of years. Clearly, I cannot claim to speak for all of them, for there are among Hispanics many varieties and shades of opinion. But I also cannot speak without them.

However, the reason for calling attention to the story of Fuenteovejuna goes beyond a mere acknowledgment of indebtedness to colleagues and friends. It is also a call for a different style of doing theology—a Fuenteovejuna style. If theology is the task of the church, and the church is by definition a community, there should be no such thing as an individual theology. The best theology is a communal enterprise.

This is a contribution that Hispanics can bring to theology. Western theology—especially that which takes place in academic circles—has long suffered from an exaggerated individualism. Theologians, like medieval knights, joust with one another, while their peers cheer from the stands where they occupy places of honor and the plebes look at the contest from a distance—if they look at all. The methodology of a Hispanic "Fuenteovejuna" theology will contrast with this. Ours is not a tradition that values individualism, as does that of the North Atlantic.

Indeed, ours is a language that does not even have a word for that "privacy" which the dominant North American culture so values. Coming out of that tradition, our theology will result from a constant dialogue among the entire community. In the end, to the degree that it is true to the faith and experience of that community, to that very degree will it be impossible for any of us to speak of "my" theology or "your" theology. It will not be a theology of theologians but a theology of the believing and practicing community. When someone asks us, "¿Quién mató al comendador?" all we shall be able to answer is "Fuenteovejuna, señor."

CHAPTER 2

Who Are We?

When I began teaching in Atlanta, Georgia, I opened my first lecture by telling my students that there was a time when Havana—not Savannah, Georgia, but Havana, Cuba—was the capital of Georgia. And then I went on to say, "Welcome, y'all furriners." This was intended only as a joke, but it may also serve to point out a fact often forgotten: As far as time is concerned, it is not the Hispanic-American but the Anglo-American who is the newcomer to this country.[1] Nineteen years before the British founded their first colony in the land that Sir Walter Raleigh called Virginia, the Spanish based in Cuba founded a city that still exists in Saint Augustine, Florida. And twelve years before the Pilgrims landed on Plymouth Rock, the Spanish founded the city of Santa Fe, New Mexico.

Hispanics in the United States

Actually, the first Hispanics to become part of this country did not do so by migration but were rather engulfed by the United States in its process of expansion—sometimes by purchase, sometimes by military conquest, and sometimes by simple annexation of territories no one was strong enough to defend. Even without turning back to history, this is clear when one looks at a map of the United States and finds in it such names as Florida, California, Nevada, Colorado, Los Angeles, San Francisco, San Diego, Sacramento, and Key West (a corruption of "Cayo Hueso").

This process was begun in 1810, when the United States annexed western Florida in order to have an outlet into the Gulf of Mexico—at that time truly the Gulf *of Mexico*—and by 1853 the new and expanding

31

country had acquired, by various means, what is now Florida, Texas, New Mexico, Arizona, California, Nevada, Utah, and sizable parts of Colorado, Kansas, Oklahoma, and Wyoming. This included more than half of what used to be Mexico and more than doubled the territory of the United States. As is usual in such cases of imperialistic expansion, the entire process was made more palatable to the national consciousness by means of an ideology that clouded the base motives involved. In this case, it was the ideology of "manifest destiny," a phrase first heard in 1845, and one that soon captivated the American mind. The United States, it appeared, was manifestly destined by God to lead the world to progress and freedom. In 1823 President Monroe had proclaimed his famous doctrine, that the United States would not tolerate colonial ventures by foreign powers in the Western Hemisphere. In 1844 Texas became a state of the Union, thus violating the terms of the agreement between Mexico and the United States that Texas would not be annexed to the Union—so much for the myth that the United States has never broken a treaty. Then followed the war with Mexico, which had been contemplated for a long time. Already in 1836 John Quincy Adams had declared that in such a war Mexico would be fighting for liberty and the United States for slavery.[2] Later Ulysses S. Grant, who had participated in the war and who was convinced that it was the result of a conspiracy to increase the number of slave-holding states, declared that the Civil War was the punishment of God for the outrage of the war with Mexico.[3] In any case, what is important is to remember that by hook *and* crook, the United States came to possess vast lands inhabited by people of Hispanic culture. Thus in the beginning it was not Hispanics who migrated to this nation, but this nation that migrated to Hispanic lands.

This process is still remembered with bitterness by Hispanics on both sides of the border—all the more so since Anglo-Americans seem to have rewritten history so as to forget these facts. I still remember listening in anger and disbelief as an educated United Methodist layman, at the General Conference of 1972, declared with conviction that he was proud that his was the only major nation in the world that had never engaged in wars of conquest. As long as such a view of history prevails in our schools, our media, and our churches, Hispanic Americans—and Native Americans—will remain aliens in the land of their ancestors.

However, the reason for mentioning this expansionist process here is not to lay a claim on land grabbed through greed, deceit, and sheer force. There is an ancient Spanish saying: "ladrón que roba a ladrón, ha cien años de perdón" (a thief who robs a thief has a hundred years' pardon). It is clear that the means by which these territories had earlier become Spanish were no more honorable than the means by which they became part of the United States. On the basis of a first claim to these lands, no one but the Native Americans would have a right to them—and even then it would be necessary to determine which tribe was where first, and who was dispossessed by whom.

The reason why this process of conquest and annexation of Spanish territories is briefly retold here is twofold. First—a matter to which we shall return later—it is essential for understanding the feelings of many Hispanics about this country and the freedom it promises. Second, this story serves to point out that the roots of Hispanic Americans in this country are old and deep and that we therefore cannot be understood merely on the basis of the process by which various waves of immigrants have come to form part of it. Hispanic Americans have been here for so long, and yet kept their identity, that it is rather doubtful that they will follow the same process of assimilation by which Swedes, Irish, and Italians have joined the mainstream of American society.[4] Especially now that there is an increasing awareness of the value of one's culture and traditions, it seems safe to predict that Hispanic Americans will be around *mañana*, and for as many *mañanas* as it pleases God to grant to this country. If Hispanic Americans did not lose their identity when they believed in the "melting pot" view of American society, it is highly unlikely that they will lose it now when that myth has been exploded. Although there are a few Hispanic Americans—mostly among the most recent arrivals—who still believe that assimilation is possible and desirable, the vast majority—including the children of many who thought they had been assimilated—are going back to their historic roots and affirming their distinctiveness, not as something of which to be ashamed or to hide from view but as something of which to be proud and to exhibit at every possible opportunity.

Our Growing Sense of Unity

Furthermore, a few years ago Puerto Ricans in New York paid no attention to the struggles of the farm workers in California, and Cubans in Miami could not care less about the chances of Herman Badillo in New York politics, but the last few years have brought about a growing solidarity among the various groups of Hispanic Americans—a consciousness that does not yet overcome group pride and prejudice but that is nevertheless significant. This is likely to influence national politics in the future, for although Hispanics have been able to attain a measure of political strength in some of the communities where they are numerous, they have not had comparable success at the level of federal government, mostly due to a lack of coordination between the various Hispanic groups involved.[5]

This growing sense of unity among Hispanic Americans has two main foci. One could be termed the "social" focus, and the other the "cultural."

The social focus of Hispanic identity is provided by the increasing awareness among Hispanics of our meager participation as a group in the decisions that shape our lives. In 1982 the median family income among Hispanics was $16,228, while that of the "rest of the population" was $23,907.[6] This is not improving, for in terms of real dollars Hispanic income has dropped consistently since 1979. Between 1973 and 1985 the typical Hispanic family's real income declined by more than $2,000.[7] As a result, in 1985 39.9% of all Hispanic children lived below the poverty level.

Furthermore, particularly in the case of Puerto Ricans, Mexican-Americans, and Central Americans, there is a factor the census does not take account of, which if taken into account would greatly increase the poverty level of Hispanics. Many Hispanic workers send a substantial portion of their income back to Puerto Rico, Mexico, or Central America, where they support elderly parents, children, spouses, or other relatives. In 1986, for instance, it was estimated that the El Salvadoran refugee community alone sent between $300 and $500 million back to El Salvador. Thus many Hispanics have dependents who (since they do not reside in the United States) are not counted by the census—nor by the Internal Revenue Service—but who would clearly place them even further below the poverty level, if they were accounted for.

The unemployment rate among Hispanics is also significantly higher than for the rest of the population. While numbers have varied according to the fluctuations of the economy, since 1973 the ratio of Hispanic unemployment to unemployment in the rest of the population has remained fairly constant, at a rate that is approximately 150% higher for Hispanics. In 1979 this rate of unemployment began to increase significantly, and in 1981 it took an even more marked turn upward. In 1982 it reached 13.8%,[8] and it has remained generally at that level, with peak periods of higher unemployment, since that time.

These statistics are paralleled by those describing educational attainment. In 1983 58% of Hispanics 25 to 34 years of age were high school graduates, and 17% of these had gone on to finish college. This represented an improvement over similar statistics for 1970, when 45% were high school graduates and 9% had college degrees. Still, it compared unfavorably with similar statistics for the rest of the population, of which 88% were high school graduates and 28% had had four or more years of college.[9] Also, by concentrating on young adults of at least 25 years of age, these statistics do not reflect the large number of Hispanics who for economic and other reasons temporarily drop out of school and later complete a high school equivalency course. Indeed, the dropout rate among Hispanics, as well as the rate at which they lag behind their peers in school, is alarming. Hispanics drop out of school at a rate that is more than double the national rate. Also, while fewer than one in ten white students aged 14 to 20 are two or more years behind their contemporaries, the rate among Mexican-Americans and Puerto Ricans is one in four.[10]

Conditions are not much better when it comes to the standing of Hispanics in academic theology. In 1985 and 1986, only four Hispanics—Protestant and Catholic—completed a Ph.D., Th.D., or S.T.D. in a school accredited by the Association of Theological Schools.[11] In the following academic year, the total number of graduates was again four—in this case none with a Ph.D.[12] The figures for enrollment in the basic seminary degree program are much more encouraging, having risen from 264 in 1972 to 1,386 in 1987. However, even after this increase of 425% in fifteen years, Hispanics constitute only 2.5 % of seminarians, both Catholic and Protestant.[13]

Hispanics are grossly underrepresented at the managerial levels in the enterprises in which most of us are engaged. Until recently, our vote has been discounted by politicians—and still is, except in those areas where we constitute a very high proportion of the electorate. For these reasons, while we have profited from laws enacted in response to the black civil rights movement, we have also seen those laws applied less stringently in areas where we are the main object of discrimination. The Reagan administration, with its attempts at dismantling the legal and political gains made by minorities in this country, led Hispanics as well as other minorities to the painful realization that the war against institutionalized racism has barely begun, and that many hard battles are still ahead. As these lines are being written, under a new administration that uses more careful rhetoric, we still see no improvement.

Pressed by these realities, Hispanic Americans are becoming politically more astute. Some have come to the conclusion that grape and lettuce interests from California have played a part in convincing militant anticommunist Cuban exiles in Miami that the movement to unionize farm workers is somehow connected with a great Communist plot. The same interests have convinced Chicanos in California that all Cubans are reactionaries who will not support their movement. Slum lords in New York and Chicago play Puerto Ricans against other Hispanic groups. In short, the dominant minority is playing the old game of offering a small slice of the pie to one group and a carrot on a stick to another, thus keeping them divided and powerless. Therefore, Hispanic Americans are beginning to unite out of the sheer political necessity of presenting a common front against the powers that would otherwise keep us subservient. We have come to realize that we come from different countries and backgrounds, and that on many points our political outlooks differ, but also that in the present situation we must either unite or prepare to be ignored.

The same is true of our growing sense of solidarity with other minorities. When national magazines start publishing articles about Hispanics as the great minority of the next decades and declaring that we will outnumber Afro-Americans as the main minority in this country,[14] some naive Hispanics rejoice in that finally attention is being paid to them. But others realize that this is simply another instance of playing one minority against the other, and that the articles about the growing numbers and success of Hispanics are intended to be read by Afro-Americans and other minorities as "watch out, here come the Hispanics." Justice would not be served if some of the meager resources now in the hands of blacks and other minorities were put in the hands of Hispanics while the present institutionalized racism persists. Our cause, we have come to realize, is a Hispanic cause because that is who we are, but it is above all a cause of justice, because of what we are all called to be.

And let us not deceive ourselves into believing that the games mentioned above are played only in "secular" society. In churches, church agencies, church colleges, and seminaries, the same games are played. A portion of the budget, a number of positions, or a few courses in a curriculum are reserved for "minority concerns," and then we are encouraged to fight it out, as if our struggle were against one another and not against the basic injustices of the present order.

The cultural focus of Hispanic-American identity is obviously the Spanish language and the culture associated with it. For years, language was seen by many as the great barrier impeding social progress. The church joined in this understanding, and until recently there were church-owned schools where it was forbidden to speak Spanish, on the grounds that the school was attempting to introduce its students into the mainstream of American society—although one suspects that at least as important a reason was that teachers felt threatened by students who could communicate in a language they did not understand. Parents spoke their broken English at home, in the hope of thus giving their children a better chance in life. Since all formal education took place in

English, in many communities Spanish was lost as an instrument of precise communication and remained only as the less developed language in which one could express only those things learned in the cradle—things that, although less sophisticated, are nevertheless the most important elements in human life. The result was that Hispanics, lacking contact with the best artistic and intellectual achievements of Spanish and Latin American culture and finding their language a limited means of expression, were tempted to believe the disparaging things said about them and their culture in the media, in the way history was taught, and in the way society was organized.

All this is now passing. Younger generations of Hispanic Americans, spurred by the examples of Afro-Americans and other minorities, are turning to their cultural roots. They are insisting on college courses taught in Spanish. They are demanding bilingual public education, not as a remedial program for those who do not know English but as a means of highlighting the values and advantages of biculturalism.[15] And in this process they are becoming increasingly aware of the North Atlantic tribalism that has characterized this country. They ask, for instance, why is it that in a series entitled *The Annals of America*[16] such "annals" include so little of the Hispanic tradition in this country? Why is it that Spanish art, literature, and history are hardly known in this country, as compared not only with those of Britain but also with those of France and Germany? Even the name "America" raises the question: What preposterous conceit allows the inhabitants of a single country to take for themselves the name of an entire hemisphere? What does this say about that country's view of those other nations who share the hemisphere with it?[17]

This process of cultural awakening must be seen as a positive development. By going back to their cultural roots, younger generations of Hispanic Americans are gaining a new sense of identity and dignity. They are being liberated to be themselves and to determine their own future by their own values and standards, and not by goals set by others. This may be threatening to many. It will certainly be dangerous, for freedom always involves a risk. But without such freedom and risk it is impossible to be the full human beings God intends us to be.

This does not mean, however, that an awakening of Hispanic culture is to be equated with the liberation God is bringing about in today's world. Culture can be very liberating for those who feel oppressed by values and standards set by others. But there is a certain understanding of "culture" that is little more than another means of oppression. Thus understood, "culture" is the entire set of values and standards that the

37

ruling groups set up in order to authenticate their own power and to keep the rest subservient. "Culture" develops at the high point of power of a nation or a group. The high point of Spanish culture, the *siglo de oro*, was also the high point of Spanish imperialism, and that culture— including Spanish religion—was used to subjugate the supposedly un-cultured people who inhabited this hemisphere. Therefore, although today in this country Hispanic culture may well be a liberating and dignifying counter-culture, we Hispanic Americans must not forget that this very culture was developed and sifted by the pharaohs of the sixteenth and seventeenth centuries.[18] From our tradition, we may gain some significant insights into the meaning of the gospel, and we may offer those insights to others. But let us not so idolize our culture that we oppress another Hispanic who does not speak as we do, or even one who never learned how to speak Spanish, because the pressures of society were too great. What will be most important in our attempts to rediscover the original liberating gospel will not be our participation in Spanish culture but our participation, jointly with the early church, with Jesus and the apostles, and with Afro-Americans and Asian Americans, in the condition of a dispossessed minority whom God is calling to new life. It is from this perspective that Christian theology must be rewritten.

While the cultural focus of Hispanic identity is exclusively our own, the social focus is something we share with many others in this country. It is for this reason that I have decided to write this essay in English. Written in Spanish, it would have addressed the Hispanic community almost exclusively. It would thus have run the risk of contributing to the distance among minorities that has been described above and that is one of the main reasons why the ruling minority is seldom challenged in its power and prejudice. Written in English, I hope that it may serve to surface some of the common concerns and perspectives that Hispanics share with blacks, women, and other underrepresented groups.

Beyond Innocence

When the layman whom I have already mentioned stood at the General Conference of the United Methodist Church and proudly declared that the United States is the only major world power that has not engaged in wars of territorial expansion, he innocently believed what he said. Such innocence, however, does not render one guiltless. It is, on the contrary, a guilty innocence. It is not the innocence of sinless Eden but rather the innocence of Adam and Eve trying to hide their nakedness behind fig leaves and ultimately hoping to hide from a reckoning with truth. It is the innocence of guilt so deep and so threatening that one cannot deal with it and therefore seeks to suppress it.

American history, as taught in our schools and even to a degree in our universities, is guilty of such innocence. The Pilgrim "Fathers"— one seldom hears of the mothers—came to this land in quest of religious freedom, and that is the reason why from its very outset this has been a land of freedom. That most of the early settlers denied that freedom to any who disagreed with them is mentioned but is not allowed to play a central role in the interpretation of events. Then the revolutionary "fathers" sued for independence, mostly in the name of freedom. That this was to a great degree the freedom to make money and to take lands from the Indians is again mentioned but is not allowed to play more than a secondary role in our understanding of the "revolutionary" war. (I sometimes wonder what would happen today if Hispanics and other minorities were to refuse to pay taxes under the principle of "no taxation without representation.") We seldom hear of the degree to which the leaders of the movement for independence lusted for Indian lands that the British would not allow them to possess. Perhaps we hear of the saga of the Cherokees and the Trail of Tears. But we are not allowed to see that this, rather than an unfortunate and isolated mistake, was simply a clear example of what took place again and again. The West was "won," we are told. But how, and who "lost" it, is not part of our national consciousness. And then we are told of the great economic expansion into world markets, of American investments overseas, and of our defense of freedom in distant lands. But we are not told that often what our soldiers were unwittingly defending was the investment of our corporations.

All this, and more, we have not been told. But let us not deceive ourselves. We have not been told because we did not wish to be told. We have rejected any who would draw attention to these and other facts as "muckrakers," and with that we have remained satisfied. But it is precisely in that willful innocence that guilt lies. For the reason why we did not wish to be told was not, as we claim, respect for our dead heroes. The reason why this country has refused to hear the truth in its own history is that as long as it is innocent of such truth, it does not have to deal with the injustices that lie at the heart of its power and its social order. If the Pilgrims, the patriots, and the pioneers were pure and just, they must have created a pure and just order, and it is our great fortune to have inherited it, and our task to defend it. Anything else is ingratitude and lack of patriotism.

Hispanics, on the other hand, have had to deal with a different sort of history. We always knew that our ancestors were not guiltless. Our Spanish ancestors took the lands of our Indian ancestors. Some of our Indian ancestors practiced human sacrifice and cannibalism. Some of our Spanish forefathers raped our Indian foremothers. Some of our Indian foremothers betrayed their people in favor of the invaders. It is not a pretty story. But it is more real than the story that white settlers came to this land with pure motivations, and that any abuse of its inhabitants was the exception rather than the rule. It is also a story resulting in a painful identity.[19]

As Hispanics, ours is a noninnocent history. We do have our heroes, from whose deeds and inspiration we draw strength. But our heroes do not wear white hats, like the Anglo heroes of the West (and, by the way, the "cowboy" is not an Anglo creation but a replica of the older Mexican *vaquero*). Sometimes some of us long for the self-assured innocence of Anglo history—To be able to claim that aside from some minor mistakes, we and our ancestors have been right! But such innocence has not been granted to us, and for that we must be thankful, for it would be a guilty innocence.

In our country, such guilty innocence is the handmaiden of injustice. Injustice thrives on the myth that the present order is somehow the result of pure intentions and a guiltless history. For instance, as long as someone can stand in a church assembly and declare with a straight face and a clear conscience that this nation has never engaged in wars of conquest—and as long as he or she is applauded for doing so, as this brother was—there is little hope that justice will be done to those whose present oppression is the result of wars that supposedly never took place. Therefore, when we seek to bring to the consciousness of our fellow citizens the enormity of the war with—perhaps it would be better to say "against"—Mexico, we do not do this out of a muckraking depravity, nor even to reclaim the lands that were taken long ago. Again, we know that "ladrón que roba a ladrón ha cien años de perdón" (a thief who steals from a thief has a hundred years' pardon). What we seek rather is to bring our fellow citizens to an acknowledgment that the present order is the result not merely of hard labor, daring enterprise, and rugged individualism but also of theft. Perhaps once we are agreed that we are all *ladrones*, it will be easier for all of us to see more clearly into issues of justice.

This is one of our functions as a Hispanic minority in this country. It is not a pleasant function, for few love those who destroy the myths by which they live. But it is a necessary function that we must courageously fulfill .

Thus to the question "Who are we?" we respond: We are those who from the beginning have had to live beyond the myth of innocence.

By the Waters of Babylon

Finally, Hispanics in this country are a people in exile. Many of us are exiles in the literal, everyday sense. For some reason, we have left our native lands and come to this land. Some of us are political exiles. We are here, in the immediate sense, because we disagreed with the political regime in our countries and the United States offered us refuge—or, in the case of those of us fleeing from right-wing dictatorships whom the United States supported, refuge was not offered, but we took it anyhow.[20] Others are economic refugees. In our lands it was impossible to make a decent living, so we took the opportunity earlier immigrants took and came to the United States. Others are ideological refugees. The propaganda coming out of this country was such that we became convinced that the values of this society were better than those in our own native societies and that therefore we would be more at home here. Most of us are here as a result of a combination of these factors. If, for whatever reasons, the lands of our birth are now permanently lost to us, if we no longer hope to return but have cast our lot in this adoptive land, we are no longer Latin Americans living in exile in the United States but Hispanic Americans, people who have no other land than this, but who nevertheless remain exiles.

Then there are many others who are not exiles in the sense that they left the lands of their birth to come to this nation. They were born here. In many cases, so were their parents and grandparents. But they too are exiles in the deeper sense of living in a land not their own. Although they are U.S. citizens by birth, they are not full citizens, and therefore they are exiles living in a land that remains foreign.

Both groups live in ambiguity. The literal exiles live in the ambiguity between gratitude and anger. We are grateful, because this country has offered us a refuge others did not. But at the same time we are angry, mostly for two reasons: first, because many of us are coming to the bitter realization that even though we have given up the countries of our birth, we shall end our days as exiles, as people who live in a land that is not theirs, that welcomes them up to a point and then shuts the door. Second, we are angry because we are becoming increasingly aware of the degree to which the United States, the land of our refuge, is also the land that created our need for exile in the first place. Political exiles discover the complicity of North American vested interests in the events that led to the need to abandon their countries. Economic exiles eventually learn that the poverty of their native lands is the result of the wealth of their adoptive land. Ideological exiles discover that the talk of freedom and equality, constantly heard overseas when it was a matter of opposing enemies of the United States, is less heard in the very land from which it comes when it is a matter of justice for ethnic minorities and for the poor.

Hispanic Americans who are native to this country also live in ambiguity. They have no other land. They never did. And yet in many ways, both tacitly and explicitly, they are being told to go home. Home? Where? They have no other home. They have never had another home. And yet this is not their home. In one's home, one is free to move the furniture around, or at least to discuss with other members of the household how the furniture ought to be arranged. But in this land, when Hispanic Americans, even those who were born here, start trying to move the furniture around, they are told to mind their own business.

This is who we are: a people in exile.[21] By the waters of Babylon we shall live and die. By the waters of Babylon we shall sing the songs of Zion. Our Zion is not the lands where we were born, though we still love them, for those lands are lost to us forever—and, in any case, since we have lived for a long time beyond innocence, we could never equate those lands with Zion. The Zion to which we sing, the Zion for which we hope, the Zion toward which we live, is the coming order of God, where all will have a vine and a fig tree under which to sit, and *none shall make them afraid* (Micah 4:4). And while we wait for that day, it may be that, as exiles, we have some insights into what it means to be a pilgrim people of God, followers of One who had nowhere to lay his head.

CHAPTER 3

The Wider Context

As we seek to develop a Hispanic theology and to implement the teaching of it in our churches and theological institutions, it is important that we place that theology in its proper historical context. As a historian of the church and its theology, I venture to suggest that historians of future centuries will speak of the "Reformation of the Twentieth Century" in terms similar to those we now employ to speak of the Reformation of the sixteenth century.[1] Indeed, we are living in a time of vast changes in the church's self-understanding, and it is possible that the consequences of those changes will be more drastic than those which took place in the sixteenth century. Hispanic theology, whose first steps we now witness, is but one element of that vast reformation and can be properly understood only when viewed within that larger context.

Events and Macroevents

Historians have amply shown that the Reformation of the sixteenth century took place within the context of a series of new circumstances of which the main protagonists of the Reformation were at best only dimly aware. Likewise, the reformation of the twentieth century is taking place in the setting of a series of "macroevents"—events so large and far-reaching that we only become aware of them when we stand back from daily events and try to see the trends of the last few centuries.

The first of these macroevents has been recognized repeatedly, although the church seems reluctant to take its implications seriously. It is the end of the Constantinian era. Ever since the fourth century, the church has existed in politically and socially advantageous conditions. Although there has always been an undercurrent of critical opposition—

mostly in the monastic tradition—Christianity has been allied with the existing order of society and has profited from it. The French Revolution, the revolutions of 1848, the Russian Revolution, and more recent developments in Latin America and other parts of the world have eroded that position of advantage. In some areas, Christians have reacted with a nostalgic attempt to return to a real or fictitious past. This is clearly the case in the United States, whose process of "de-Constantinization" has been slower than that of many other countries, and where the New Right defends the old wrongs in the name of "Christian civilization." Among Roman Catholics, the Opus Dei movement and other movements like it display a similar mentality. It seems clear that these are rearguard skirmishes. The protagonists may win an election or two. They may even hope to turn the United States into a fascist state. But in terms of long-range history, they are already defeated.

A second macroevent, closely associated with the first in the minds of many in the southern nations, is the failure of the North. As we look at microevents, we are inclined to believe that we are living in a time of great confrontation between East and West. The big questions in our newspapers seem to be how the Soviets will behave, who will be our next president, and whether it is the Russians or the United States who have the largest nuclear arsenal. But we must not allow these questions to obscure the macroevent of the promises of the North in the nineteenth century, which the twentieth has found to be false. The nineteenth century was a time when leading minds all over the world expected the West—which was really the North Atlantic—to usher in a new era of prosperity for humankind. In Latin America, for instance, Bolívar and his generation looked to Great Britain, France, and the United States for guidance into the future. The first Latin American governments encouraged closer ties with the Western powers as the only way to develop their nations and raise the standard of living of their citizens. (In passing, it may be said that this mood contributed significantly to the establishment of the earliest Protestant missions in Latin America, as well as to Protestant immigration into that continent.) This attitude was also present in the North Atlantic, where people spoke of the "white man's burden" of taking civilization, Christianity, and material welfare—all wrapped into one—to the poorer nations of the world.

In a way, the Russian Revolution was a belated stage of the promises of the North. What Russia promised was the beginning of a new age in which, under her leadership, justice and material prosperity would sweep the world. Like the other promises of the North, this too found willing ears in the South, and throughout the poorer nations there were those who devoted their lives to the fulfillment of the dream from

Russia. It eventually became apparent, however, that Russian leaders were as imperialistic as any, that they shared with the rest of the North the dream of universal hegemony, and that therefore to escape subservience to the West—really, the Northwest—by submitting to the East—really, the Northeast—was not a happy prospect. It is for this reason that the pro-Russian Communist parties in the South, so dreaded by the CIA, have very little appeal in the poorer nations and are generally discounted as irrelevant by most leaders of the left.

The promises of the North did materialize to a measure and for a time. Medical science, literacy, agricultural techniques, transportation, and general technological knowledge were the great contribution of the North to the nations of the South. These have left their mark, and their gift cannot be denied. In fact, it was the success of the North in these areas that gave its promises credibility for a time—and even today. As a second-century Christian writer commented, error must clothe itself in truth in order to have power.[2]

But at another level these promises have turned sour. Take, for instance, the development of agriculture through new techniques and machinery and through the creation of transportation facilities to take products to worldwide markets. These inspired high expectations of economic improvement for the masses in the southern countries. But the net result has been the growth of export crops and increasing hunger and political instability in the countries supposedly "developing" along those lines. To speak of the present system of land tenure and agricultural production in Latin America as a remnant of "medieval feudalism," as some do, is to misrepresent the facts. The present system is the result of the "development" of the nineteenth and early twentieth centuries, following the blueprints provided by the development of the North. For instance, the present unrest in Central America is closely related to the fact that vast areas of land previously devoted to producing food for the native population have been diverted to the production of beef and fruit for export. Had the land not been "developed," its monetary value would be less, and the titleless peasants would have been allowed to continue tilling it. But now, with roads, railways, refrigeration, and the like, the land has become part of the worldwide economy, and the peasants, pushed off of the land, have become poorer while the "country"—that is, its ruling classes—has become richer. In the Philippines, land held for generations by peasants without legal documents has been bulldozed and plowed for the mass production of pineapples—by American companies fleeing the unionization of their laborers in Hawaii—thus increasing both the GNP of the country and the misery of its masses.[3] Such examples could be multiplied ad infinitum. But the point is simply that one of the macroevents of our time is that the masses of the world are experiencing the failure of the promises of the North in a very painful way. To them, this is not theory but tragedy. One could say that, as was also true of the German peasants of the sixteenth century who eventually revolted, what we are witnessing is not merely the continuation of earlier injustice but its increase.

The conflict between East and West, which so dominates our view of world events, thus becomes simply another instance—perhaps the greatest instance—of the failure of the North. What used to be called Western civilization but was in truth North Atlantic civilization is now divided between East and West. Both are equally part of the North that has failed to deliver. And both are now exporting their mutual animosity to the South, which they have turned into the main battlefield for a war that would be too costly were it to be waged in the North.

The nuclear arms race is further proof of the failure of the North. The "white men" whose burden it was to save humankind have now led us to the brink of destruction and seem unable to stop their runaway military technology—fueled, at least in the West, by the many economic interests that profit from the hysterical arms buildup, justified on the basis of a so-called window of vulnerability. The two colossi of the North have been aptly compared to two people standing waist-high in a pool of gasoline, arguing over who has more matches. This is hardly a picture to inspire confidence in the South or to justify the position of leadership that the North has enjoyed for the last decades.

Oddly enough, the failure of the North is to be seen also in what many consider the greatest sign of its success: the vast numbers who seek to immigrate into it. At first glance, the masses who cross the Rio Grande every day and the countless others who would like to do so are the clearest sign of the value and success of North American capitalism. They are, as some would say, "voting with their feet" for the economic and political order of the United States. But this is so only from a limited perspective. When one remembers that American and Northern European capitalism was announced as the hope of humankind, and particularly when one takes into account that it has had its way in Latin America for over a century, the masses seeking to cross the border are not so much a vindication as an indictment of a system that has not worked. If, after a century and a half of Northern neocolonialism in the South, conditions there are such that people seek to leave the homeland that they love, this shows not that the system is so good but that it results in gross inequities between the colonizer and the colonized. It is true that many in this great migratory wave, as well as those others on this side of the border who seek to stop it, do not see the connection between the "development" of the North and the "misdevelopment" of the South, and that for such people the pressure being exerted on the border is a sign of the success of the North. Indeed, the notion that the North is successful while the South is a failure lies at the root of the struggle of many Hispanics in this country with their own identity. But an economic analysis of the entire situation shows a relation of cause and effect so that our presence in this country is not a sign of the success of the North but rather of its failure, for it has been able to succeed only on the basis of misdeveloping the South.

A third macroevent of our time is the growing self-consciousness of many who were mostly silent until fairly recent times. In a measure, this is the response of the South to the failure of the North. But it goes far beyond that. A few decades ago, Christian missionary leaders spoke of the decline of ancient world religions, of their loss of vitality, and of their eventual disappearance. Some even hoped for what amounted to a new Constantinian era in China, Japan, and some areas of Africa. But now we see the resurgence of Islam as both a political and a religious power. While European and North American Christian theologians were speaking of a "secular age," they were mystified at the sight of Buddhist monks burning themselves to death for their beliefs, ayatollahs coming to power in Iran, and the lethargic Roman Catholic Church in Latin America becoming involved in the struggle of the poor for social justice. Many North American citizens are shocked, dismayed, and angered at a United Nations organization where the "Big Powers" no longer hold power. With typical Northern myopia, they blame Russia for this, when the truth is that Russia too is among the powers that are losing their authority.

This third macroevent, however, goes far beyond a North-South issue. In the North as well as in the South, people who have been silent for generations are now speaking up and claiming an authority that past centuries have denied them.

One aspect of this is the growing class awareness of many, both in the South and in the North. In Latin America, for instance, it has become commonplace to speak of many of those whom authorities in the United States consider "Latin American leaders"—those whom U.S. presidents visit in their "good-will" tours—as "Herodians," that is, as local citizens who in truth serve foreign powers. For the oppressed classes in the South, the present North-South struggle takes concrete shape in their struggle against such Herodians—and these include not only political figures but also industrialists, and any who would sell the patrimony of the poor for greater profit.

In various settings, this third macroevent takes the form of growing self-consciousness on the part of ethnic minorities. A well-known example is that of Afro-Americans in the United States, who in recent decades have made it clear that they will no longer derive their self-understanding from what the dominant culture tells them. The motto "Black is beautiful" expresses this quite well. Similar movements are taking place among blacks in various parts of the world, among Indians in Latin America, among "mountain people" in Taiwan and "barakumin" in Japan, and among several ethnic minorities in the USSR. All of these groups, while agreeing that class issues are an important aspect of their struggle, refuse to allow everything to be reduced to class struggle—which after all is another white, Northern analysis of the human situation.

Likewise, women, who like children have been told that they are to be "seen but not heard," are also raising their voices. All over the world, they are speaking with a forcefulness unheard of a generation ago. In various countries and cultures, this takes different forms—and white North Atlantic women are frequently reminded by their darker sisters that their experience is both feminine *and* white, and that they are therefore both sisters and oppressors.[4] This may lead some observers to the mistaken conclusion that the women's movement is essentially a white or a middle-class movement. But the truth is that, united or in disagreement with one another, women throughout the world are speaking up, demanding their place in the scheme of things. This is a significant element in the third macroevent that I am describing: Those who were silent are now demanding to be heard, and making themselves heard.

In short, those whose opinions and contributions have been rejected for reasons of class, nationality, sex, age, sexual orientation, and the like, will no longer be silent. This is a macroevent of enormous proportions, for it means that the vast majority of humankind, until now resigned to be followers because this seemed to be their place in the general scheme of things, is insisting on its right to have its share both in the ordering of life and in the bounties of the earth. The present distribution of power and wealth is seen as unjust by a growing portion of the world's population. This is a macroevent that cannot be ignored.

The Reformation of the Twentieth Century

The Reformation of the sixteenth century was shaped by the macroevents of that time—the end of the Byzantine Empire, rising nationalism in western Europe, the Renaissance, Humanism, discovery and colonization of new lands, and so on. Likewise, the reformation of the twentieth century is taking place within the context of the macroevents of our time, and several of its characteristics reflect those macroevents.

One characteristic of our macroreformation is that voices are being heard from quarters that have not been the traditional centers of theological inquiry, and from people who have not been among the traditional theological leaders. When mission theoreticians in past decades spoke of the "three selfs" as a goal for younger churches, they included self-support, self-government, and self-propagation. They did not envision self-interpretation or self-theologizing. They expected theology to continue being what it was, for the meaning of the gospel was fully understood by the sending churches, and all that the younger ones had to do was continue proclaiming the same message. At best, these younger churches were to recast the message in terms of their own culture. The surprise of our generation has been that the younger churches have provided insights into the meaning of the gospel and the mission of the church that the older churches sorely needed. From Asia, Africa, and Latin America, as well as from ethnic minorities in North America and in other places, and from women all over the world, have come stunning visions of the meaning of the gospel, and a number of theologians in the traditional centers of theological learning have seen the value of these insights. The dialogue that has resulted means that theology will never be the same again.

There is a misconception in some quarters that this implies a disparagement of theological scholarship. This is not so. Nobody is more aware of the value of theological scholarship than are the leaders of the new emerging theology. One must be able to substantiate one's claims, particularly if they seem radically new, on the basis of solid biblical exegesis, historical research, and cogent argument. But just as Luther declared that a Christian with the Bible has more authority than the pope or a council against it, so are these new theologians convinced that a Christian community living out good news to the poor has more authority than the most learned theological faculty where such good news is not heard.

A second characteristic of our macroreformation is its conviction that the post-Constantinian era, far from being something to be feared, is leading us to a deeper understanding of the biblical message. Scripture is better understood from the perspective of the early church than from that of the Constantinian church. The meaning of the Exodus and of the law that springs from it is best understood by those who have an experience of slavery and a long trek through the wilderness. The minority report of the prophets is best understood by those who are not usually included in the chronicles of the kings or of high society. The exile is best understood by those who live in societies that are not theirs, and who "by the rivers of Babylon" are called upon to sing the songs of the Lord in a foreign land. The enormity of the self-marginalization of God in Galilee is best understood by modern-day outsiders in modern-day Galilees—ghettos, barrios, and the misdeveloped countries.[5] The post-Constantinian era, by forcing poverty and weakness upon the church, calls it to a renewed commitment to the paradoxical "good news" of the cross. At this point one is reminded of Luther's contrast between a "theology of glory" and a "theology of the cross."[6] A theology of glory attempts to see God in power, in wisdom, in happiness and prestige. It is a theology that sounds good. But it is not proper theology. A theology of the cross, on the contrary, sees God in suffering, in weakness, and in folly. A Constantinian theology will necessarily be a theology of glory. It is theology written in endowed chairs and preached from prestigious pulpits. The new theology, even when it finds its way to such chairs and pulpits, is aware that they represent a dying age, and that the coming one, although painful, will provide the church with greater opportunities for faithfulness.

A third characteristic of this macroreformation is that it looks to Scripture not only for "truth" but also for its understanding of the nature of truth. Too much traditional theology has bought into the Eleatic-Platonic understanding of truth as that which is changeless and universal, and then has sought such truths in the Bible. The new reformation believes that our understanding of the nature of truth must be such that the particular man Jesus, at a particular time and place, can say, "I am the truth." Biblical truth, the truth in which the people of God are called to live, the new reformers say, is concrete, historical truth. It does not exist in a world of pure ideas but rather is closely bound with bread and wine, with justice and peace, with a coming Reign of God—a Reign not over pure ideas or over disembodied souls but over a new society and a renewed history.

In consequence, the present macroreformation calls for a new understanding of orthodoxy as closely linked to orthopraxis.[7] To believe the truth means to live in the truth, and this means to be in love and justice with our neighbors, both near and far. The theme of justice is then heard, not only in its more traditional context of social ethics but also when speaking of the doctrine of the Trinity, of creation, of anthropology, of sacraments, of eschatology, and so on. An orthodox doctrine of the Trinity, for instance, must lead one not only to affirm the three persons and one substance but also to live the proper relations demanded by such a Trinitarian God. (There will be more on this subject in a later chapter).

In some ways, it is precisely for this reason that it is possible to speak of a new reformation. The Reformation of the sixteenth century, although centering on the basic issues of justification by grace through faith and of the authority of Scripture, soon led Christians to raise anew an entire series of theological questions that many had taken to be forever settled. Likewise, but in an even more radical manner, the theology that is developing in the context of the macroevents of our time is asking questions not only about justice, important as that is, but also about every other theological subject. The church and the systems of doctrine emerging from such a process will be radically different from what we have known in recent centuries—probably to such a point that the changes of the sixteenth century will seem small by comparison.

This leads us to the fourth characteristic of the present reformation: It is radically ecumenical. The issues of the sixteenth century, important as they are, are no longer seen as the crucial theological issues. When salvation, for instance, is seen in a manner different from the way in which it was seen in the sixteenth century, one comes to the realization that the positions of both Catholics and Protestants were based on a common understanding of salvation that must be corrected, and in consequence the debate regarding faith and works is posed in a manner that may well bypass the differences of the sixteenth century. At the same time, by thus posing the issues in a different manner, it is possible that the new theology will be able to do justice to some of the basic concerns of parties on both sides of the debate.[8] Furthermore, the emphasis on orthopraxis gives theological undergirding for collaboration among various ecclesiastical communities that may not be in total agreement as to the content of orthodoxy.

This ecumenism, however, does not see as its primary goal the unity of the church or the improvement of relations between churches. Such goals are important, for they are intimately related to the mission of the church. But the goal of this ecumenism is the *oikoumene*, the entire inhabited earth, over which God's Reign will come, and which the meek will receive as their inheritance. Therefore, one of the marks of the new theology is that it is not afraid to enter into dialogue and collaboration with the many movements, ideologies, parties, and programs that long for the day when the beatitudes shall be fulfilled, the poor shall receive their inheritance, and those who hunger after justice shall be filled.

The fifth and final characteristic of our reformation that I wish to point out is that, oddly enough, the emerging theology is posing anew the old medieval question of the nature of universals. In characteristic fashion, this question is not being asked in purely logical or philosophical terms but rather in terms of justice, power, and human relations. The new theology, being done by those who are aware of their traditional voicelessness, is acutely aware of the manner in which the dominant is confused with the universal. North Atlantic male theology is taken to be basic, normative, universal theology, to which then women, other minorities, and people from the younger churches may add their footnotes. What is said in Manila is very relevant for the Philippines. What is said in Tübingen, Oxford, or Yale is relevant for the entire church. White theologians do general theology; black theologians do black theology. Male theologians do general theology; female theologians do theology determined by their sex. Such a notion of "universality" based on the present unjust distribution of power is unacceptable to the new theology. If the nature of truth is as has been described above, both in its historical concreteness and in its connection with orthopraxis, it follows that every valid theology must acknowledge its particularity and its connection with the struggles and the vested interests in which it is involved. A theology that refuses to do this and that leaps to facile claims of universal validity will have no place in the postreformation church of the twenty-first century.

This, however, leaves us in a difficult position, similar to that of the extreme nominalists of the Middle Ages. Their difficulty was that if universals have no reality beyond the mind, thought has no correspondence to reality, and all statements are so particular as to be meaningless. Our present-day problem is that if theology is always concrete and expresses particular struggles and vested interests, all communication between various segments of the church becomes impossible. This is clearly not the case. The taped conversations on the Bible of a group of fisherfolk on Lake Managua, translated and published in English,[9] became a best seller in the United States and in other parts of the world, where people involved in similar but very different struggles responded to, even if they did not always agree with, what these fisherfolk saw in Scripture. A sermon by a black preacher in South Africa is received with a loud "Amen" by Asian-American women in California. The insights of an Afro-American theologian are translated into a variety of languages spoken in the poorer nations of the world. Clearly, there is a universality to these very concrete and particular theological expressions. Yet this is not the universality of abstraction but rather a very different sort of universality that is achieved, paradoxically enough, by being very concrete.

The paradox, however, surprises only those who seek to answer the question of universality and particularity after the fashion of Plato's

Parmenides, as if it were first of all a logical problem. Those, on the other hand, who start from the biblical understanding of truth know that at the heart of that understanding stands the supreme instance of this paradox: the incarnation of God in Jesus Christ. This "scandal of particularity," to borrow a phase from Kierkegaard, must not be denied by Christian theology. Thus what we see in our present paradox between the concreteness of the theology of the new reformation and its universal validity stems from the very nature of a truth at the heart of which stands the scandal of particularity. It is precisely by acknowledging and affirming their particularity that the various expressions of the new theology have a claim to universality.

There is a very practical conclusion to be drawn from the foregoing. That is the manner in which we as Hispanics should respond to those, particularly in schools of theology, who react to our desire for more input into the entire theological enterprise by saying that they have to balance our claims with those of women, Afro-Americans, and other minorities. A very natural reaction would be to try to show that our concerns are at least as important as those of blacks, women, and others. This is certainly true. But to argue in this fashion is to accept the definition of the problem that the "normative" theology of the majority—which is in fact a minority—imposes on us. There are three basic errors in that understanding of the situation. The first is to take for granted that theology as it is now taught is "general," nonethnic theology, whereas what we seek is a "particular" input. The second is to take for granted that the interests of one minority will necessarily be opposed to the interests of another. The third is to believe that a school of theology has more "universal" significance when it avoids being tied down to a concrete historical and geographical setting.

As we press the issue of Hispanic concerns in the theological enterprise, we do not seek to substitute Hispanic dominance for white dominance. Nor should we allow ourselves to be used in order to push other minority concerns to the background. On the contrary, what we seek, jointly with all others who are speaking the words of the new reformation, is to call the entire church to obedience, and to bring whatever insight we may have to the theological task of the church as a whole.

53

CHAPTER 4

Hispanics in the New Reformation

The previous chapter sought to place Hispanic experience and theology within the context of some larger events and trends in our time, first in the world at large and then in the church and its theology. We must now focus more directly on Hispanic religious history and our present situation, in order to see how those wider events relate to our own concrete task.

Our Catholic Background

Perhaps the best starting point is the question of how Hispanics view the end of the Constantinian era, and how it affects us and our faith. The Spanish-American Roman Catholic Church is part of the common background of all Hispanics—if not personally, then at least in our ancestry. Most of us were born within that church and still belong to it. Others were Protestants from the time of birth. Many, born Roman Catholics, are now Protestants. Still others have no ecclesiastical connection whatsoever. But still, somewhere in our common background, there stands the Spanish-American Roman Catholic Church.

It is very difficult for Protestants—and even for Roman Catholics—in the United States to have an idea of the changes that have taken place in Latin American Catholicism during our lifetime. You need to have experienced your classmates' crossing themselves when they learned that you were a Protestant. You need to have been invited by the more devout of those classmates to come with them to "hear mass" (people didn't normally take communion; they didn't even "go" to mass—they "heard" mass). You need to have heard a former Catholic seminarian tell of being taken to the garden, being ordered to pull up the carrots and plant them upside down, and being punished when he protested, because he had not learned the meaning of obedience. You need to have seen the bones of the poor, whose relatives could not pay for a plot of holy ground at $300 a yard, piled six feet high in an abandoned building. You need to have seen schools where poor children who received scholarships wore a uniform different from the one worn by those who paid their tuition. You need to have seen bishops and cardinals routinely blessing the works of tyrants, while the people bled to death. Then you would have some idea of the magnitude of the changes that have taken place. Then you would have understood the prejudices of a Protestant student who, four weeks into a course on the history of Christian thought, asked me when we would leave behind all this "Catholic stuff" and begin dealing with "Christian" thought. Then you would be able to begin to understand the astounding and grateful amazement with which I and my generation of Protestants look at the new Catholic Church in Latin America.

And yet, we should not be so astounded. We should not be so astounded, first, for theological reasons. We have always said and believed that unexpected things take place whenever Scripture is read anew and seriously. We are now seeing it happen, and we are discovering and having to confess that our prejudices did not agree with our theology. But second, and this is my main point, we would not have been so astounded had we realized that the apparently monolithic Catholic Church in Latin America had been two churches from the very beginning.

Few North Americans are aware of the degree to which the Catholic Church in Latin America was an arm of the powers of conquest, colonialism, and oppression. Even fewer are aware of the other reality, the underside of that Church, which repeatedly decried and opposed those powers.

Let us look first at the "topside," at the official organization of the Church and the manner in which it served the interests of conquest and colonization. From the very beginning of the conquest, the Spanish crown had over the Church in the colonies the power of "royal patronage," or *Patronato real*. Alexander VI, who apparently did not wish to be bothered with all the new lands to be evangelized when there were so many exciting developments taking place in Italy, issued a series of bulls[1] in which he granted the Spanish crown both political and religious authority over all lands discovered or to be discovered beyond a line of demarcation one hundred leagues west of the Azores, as long as they were reached sailing west and they did not already belong to a Christian ruler. Similar arrangements were already in force for Portuguese discoveries and were adapted to bring the rights of the Portuguese *Padroado* to the same level as the Spanish *Patronato*. By 1501, and probably earlier,[2] the tithes and offerings from the Church in the colonies were administered by the crown, which in turn was responsible for all expenses of the Church in the colonies.[3] When the first episcopal sees were established, Pope Julius II, who scarcely had time for his Italian wars, granted the Spanish crown the "right of presentation," whereby the crown was to "present" before the Holy See the names of those to be appointed as bishops and other high clerics in the colonies.[4] Eventually, the theory would develop, particularly among Spanish jurists, that what the popes had granted the Spanish crown was actually a "vicariate," so that the king was the pope's vicar in the New World.[5]

The attitude of the crown toward the Indians was ambivalent. On the one hand, the entire enterprise of conquest and colonization was based on deriving benefits from Indian labor. There is ample proof that the crown wished the Indians to be Christianized, not only for the benefit of their souls but also for the benefit of Spanish (or Portuguese) rule. On the other hand, the exploitation of the Indians could lead to the establishment of vast estates—practically independent empires—in the New World. Spain's unification had recently been achieved after a prolonged struggle with noble potentates who resisted the authority of the crown. Therefore, in order to prevent similar events in the New World, the Spanish sovereigns often became the defenders of the rights of Indians.[6]

The same ambivalence existed in the Church. Bishops were appointed by the crown, usually not on the basis of their pastoral experience in the New World or their love for their Indian flocks but on the basis of their connections in court.[7] The diocesan clergy ministered mostly to the Spaniards who had settled in towns, and to their Indian servants. Many of these secular or diocesan priests were devout men.[8] However, others were simply priests who had failed in Spain and were looking for a new post. Such clergy had very little idea of the sufferings that the Indians were undergoing in their process of "Christianization." All that they could see were cities arising in the wilderness, churches being built, tithes collected, schools founded, civilization being brought to savages.

There was, however, another church being born in the New World. Its ministers were mostly friars—Franciscans,[9] Dominicans,[10] Jesuits,[11] and Mercedarians[12]—who had vows of poverty and obedience and who therefore were able and ready to work in places and situations in which the secular clergy would not work. Their vows of poverty allowed these missionaries to witness and often also to share the poverty and the suffering of their flocks. Therefore, it was usually the friars who became the defenders of the Indians, protesting against their mistreatment and on occasion organizing and empowering them to take control over their own lives.

The name that is most commonly known in this context is that of Bartolomé de Las Casas, who spent most of his life seeking new and better laws for the protection of the Indians.[13] Unfortunately, one suspects that the reason he is relatively well known to the English-speaking public is that his writings about the mistreatment of the Indians have been used to confirm all the anti-Spanish and anti-Catholic prejudices of such a public. What few realize is that Las Casas, far from being a lone exception in a sea of insensitivity and injustice, was the voice of an entirely different Christianity that was arising.

The names of the founders of this other Christianity are too many even to mention. But a few of the highlights would serve to illustrate the nature of this "other church" being born out of the ministry of the friars among the dispossessed.

The Dominican Antonio de Montesinos was the first to protest against the mistreatment of the Indians, and in particular against the *encomiendas*. This was a system according to which a group of Indians were *encomendados*—entrusted—to a Spaniard in order to be "civilized" and "Christianized." In exchange for such great benefits, the Indians were to work for the Spaniard. Since the *encomendero* had no investment in the Indians entrusted to him, the resultant system was in some ways worse than slavery. In any case, thanks to Montesinos's protests, and his advocacy before the court in Spain, the laws regarding the treatment of Indians were changed in 1512. This was the first of a long series of legal reforms in which the name of Las Casas appears repeatedly, but whose actual application in the New World was in fact limited.

St. Luis Beltrán,[14] the first of the Spanish missionaries to the New World to be canonized, repeatedly rebuked the Spaniards for living off the blood of the Indians. It is said that on one such occasion, when sitting at the table of an *encomendero*, his host took offense at his comments, and that St. Luis silenced his host by taking a tortilla and squeezing blood from it. Whatever the truth may be behind this legend, it does point to the undeniable fact that there was among some of the friars an often unspoken view of the conquest, and of the economic order of the colonies, which saw the entire enterprise as founded on injustice and exploitation.

The Jesuit missionaries in Paraguay have been accused of being paternalistic, when in fact much the opposite is true. In their villages, in which most of the fields and all the animals and tools were held in common, the Indians not only learned how to manage their own lives but also practiced such specialized arts as the building of organs for their churches. It certainly was not paternalism that led the Jesuits to help the Indians, menaced by the encroachment of slave hunters, to turn their smithies into arms factories and to organize themselves into an army.[15]

In Chile the Dominican Gil González de San Nicolás[16] came to the conclusion that the wars against the Indians, whose real cause was the desire to take Indian lands, were unjust, and that therefore people who profited from such wars should not receive absolution. He convinced many of his fellow Dominicans as well as a number of Franciscans. Finally, he was accused of heresy and silenced by the authorities.

This other church also found opportunity to express itself with the coming of black slaves. As in many other parts of the world, ecclesiastical authorities found very little wrong with the institution of slavery. There were among the friars, however, many who disagreed with the authorities. Since there was not much they could do to end the institution, they did all they could to change it and to expose its opposition to the gospel. Most notable in this work was St. Pedro Claver.[17] A Catalonian Jesuit who arrived at Cartagena while still a novice, young Pedro was deeply disturbed by what he saw of the "peculiar institution," of ships whose stench could be detected before they appeared on the horizon, of broken families, broken bodies, and broken lives, and he determined that he would do something about it. When the time came for him to make his final vows, he added a fourth vow to the traditional three of poverty, chastity, and obedience: *Petrus Claver, aethiopum semper servus* (Pedro Claver, forever a slave to blacks). While he was concerned for the evangelization of blacks, and it was for this ministry that he obtained permission from his order, he did much more than that. He personally took care of lepers who had been abandoned by their masters and organized the freed blacks of the city to provide relief for these and other blacks in need. On festival days, this organization provided banquets in which the guests of honor were the lepers and the beggars, many of whom were former slaves whose owners had abandoned them because they had become unable to earn their keep. He knew that he could not attack slavery per se. But he went as far as was prudent, and then a bit. It soon became well known that he would humbly greet the poorest of slaves, and that he would cross the street to avoid greeting a slave owner. He also made it known that in listening to confession he would follow the "gospel order," beginning with the slaves, then the poor, and finally the children. As to the rich and the slave owners, he was sure they could find another confessor who had time for them.

Toward the end, bedridden, unable to move, and made to lie in his filth, he thanked God for the opportunity to experience something of what his flock had experienced in the slave ships. Then the white society realized that a saint was about to leave them, and they flocked to his cell is search of relics. When practically nothing was left but his crucifix, he was ordered to relinquish it to a marquis. Then he died, the fad passed, slavery continued, and it took the Roman Church 234 years to acknowledge him a saint.

This was the other church—the church I did not know when my friends crossed themselves; the church that probably even my friends, middle-class as they were, did not know. The most fortunate of its saints, like Pedro Claver, took centuries to be acknowledged. Most others have been forgotten. And perhaps forgotten they should remain, for this is the church of the poor, the anonymous, the unrewarded.

Whatever the case may be, that other church lived on. At various points it came to the fore. In the eighteenth century José Gabriel Túpac Amaru, claiming to be the direct descendant of the royal Incas, led the Indians of upper Peru in revolt against the Spanish. He and his successor, as well as the other leaders of the rebellion, declared themselves to be true Catholics. They were aware that the hierarchy was an instrument of Spanish power. The bishop of Cuzco instructed his priests to remind the Indians of the great "reward that is promised them if they stay away from riots and rebellions, and remain faithful subjects of our Catholic King."[18] In most cities and large towns, the urban clergy, mostly diocesan and either native Spaniards or colonials of Spanish descent, organized the resistance against the rebellion. Several of them took arms against the rebels. On the other hand, many of the village and country priests supported the rebellion. A priest who had left Peru earlier, when the Jesuits were expelled from the Spanish colonies, now appeared in London trying to persuade the English government to send support to the rebels.

The Túpac Amaru rebellion was short-lived and was drowned in blood three years after it began. But a few decades later, now in Mexico, another rebellion broke out. Under the leadership of Fr. Miguel Hidalgo y Costilla and under the flag of the Virgin of Guadalupe, Mexico proclaimed its independence. The time of the end of the Spanish empire had come, and in the struggles that ensued the Church would once again be divided between a hierarchy, mostly foreign or drawn from the native aristocracy, that supported the crown, and a lower clergy that often supported the rebels.

I cannot review here that entire development. It is significant, however, that the banner under which Hidalgo and his troops fought was that of the Virgin of Guadalupe.[19] This is symptomatic, for one of the ways—probably the most important way—in which the church of the dispossessed continued its existence was through the popular piety expressed in cults such as that of the Virgin of Guadalupe.

The legend behind this cult is instructive.[20] Briefly put, it is the story of how the Virgin appeared to Juan Diego, a poor and unlearned Indian, and gave him certain instructions to be conveyed to the bishop of Mexico. The bishop would not listen until he was forced by a miracle to admit that the Virgin had indeed appeared to Juan Diego, and that he was to do as the Indian told him. Thus the Virgin of Guadalupe became a symbol of the affirmation of the Indian over against the Spanish, of the unlearned over against the learned, of the oppressed over against the oppressor.

When I was growing up, I was taught to think of such things as the Virgin of Guadalupe as pure superstition. Therefore, I remember how surprised I was at the reaction of a Mexican professor in seminary when one of my classmates made some disparaging remarks about Guadalupe. The professor, who was as Protestant as they come and who often stooped because he was then elderly, drew himself up, looked my friend in the eye, and said: "Young man, in this class you are free to say anything you please. You may say anything about me. You certainly are welcome to say anything you wish about the pope and the priests. But don't you touch my little Virgin!"

At that time, I took this to be an atavism of an old man who had been fed superstition in his mother's milk. But now I know better. What he was saying was that, in spite of all that our North American friends had told us, in spite of the veneer of superstition, in spite of the horrendous things that took place every Sunday morning as people crawled to the shrine of Guadalupe, there was in there a kernel of truth that was very dear to his heart—and all the dearer, since so much of the religiosity that he knew, both Catholic and Protestant, denied it.[21] For generation upon generation of oppressed Indian people, told by word and deed that they were inferior, the Virgin has been a reminder that there is vindication for the Juan Diegos. And that is indeed part of the gospel message, even if it has not always been part of our own message.[22]

So we should not be too surprised by what has taken place in the Catholic Church in Latin America in recent decades: that Juan Diego has come forth, and many of the bishops have finally believed him; that the other Catholic Church, the church of Las Casas and Montesinos and Pedro Claver, has come to the fore, and that it is forcing the entire church catholic to listen to it. Also, we should not be surprised that the struggle goes on; that the Catholic Church in Latin America does not speak with one voice; that for every Archbishop Romero whose primary concern is for the people, there are a host whose primary concern is for the institutional church.

Thus from its very beginning, Spanish-American Roman Catholicism has been torn between a hierarchical church that has generally represented the powerful and stood by them and a more popular church, formed by the masses and led by pastors who have ministered at the very edge of disobedience.

This duality has been part of the experience of Roman Catholicism for most Hispanics, for it has continued long after the end of the colonial period. In the United States southwest, it is typified by Antonio José Martínez, the "cura de Taos." Martínez had prepared for the priesthood both in Mexico and in Spain and had founded Catholic churches in Peñasco, Abiquiú, Santa Fe, Cañada de Santa Cruz, Tomé, Old Messilla, and, finally, Taos. There he built a school, brought in a printing press from old Mexico, started the first newspaper, and developed a reputation as a saint. He did not believe in celibacy and was openly married. His wife was commonly known as "Madre Teodorita" and was widely respected in the community as the priest's companion. They lived at the time of the Mexican-American war and the Civil War. Through all these conflicts, Fr. Martínez guided his flock and kept it together. When New Mexico came under American rule, he was accused of resisting that rule and of abetting an uprising in Taos in which the American governor was killed. Apparently, such accusations, which were never taken to court, were not true. The truth was that Fr. Martínez repeatedly defended his people against the depredations of the newcomers, and that therefore the latter suspected him of hostile intentions.

Fr. Martínez did clash with the newly appointed bishop of Santa Fe, Jean Baptiste Lamy. Lamy, a member of the American hierarchy, was convinced that Spanish Catholicism left much to be desired. He conceived of his task as consisting partly in Americanizing his Hispanic flock. He apparently had little understanding of the problems that this flock was encountering under the new order—he counted Kit Carson among his friends and could never understand why his Hispanic flock objected. He certainly could not accept this married priest who lived openly with his wife and children. When Bishop Lamy insisted that Hispanic priests collect tithes from their parishioners, Martínez refused to do so on the grounds that his flock was already poor enough and that the business of the Church was not to collect money from the poor but rather to give it to them. For a long time, he continued ministering at the edge of obedience. Eventually, he either was excommunicated or resigned, but he refused to give up his church or his ministry. To the people in Taos, he was still their priest, and this was their church. With him went a number of other priests, and they helped him organize an independent Catholic church that was particularly strong in northern New Mexico. To this day, his name is venerated among the older Hispanic stock in New Mexico, stories still circulate of miracles connected with him and his companions, his descendants proudly claim him as an ancestor, and his tomb in Taos is a place of pilgrimage for the few who remember him.[23] At the same time, at the very center of Santa Fe, by the cathedral, stands a statue of Jean Baptiste Lamy.

Hispanics, no matter whether Catholic or Protestant, and no matter whether or not they have heard of Bartolomé de Las Casas or the cura de Taos, have been shaped by this dual Catholicism, a Catholicism that is deeply pained by the tension within itself and that is best epitomized in the common phrase—almost a contradiction for Catholics of other traditions—"soy católico, pero no creo en los curas" (I am a Catholic, but I don't believe in priests). This is not, as is often thought, a blanket anticlericalism, after the fashion of the French Revolution. It is rather a statement that only those priests who live up to their vocation, after the fashion of the "cura de Taos," are believable priests. Authority does not reside in priesthood in the hierarchical sense but rather in Catholicism—in Catholicism understood as the faith of the people and not as the monopoly of the hierarchy.

In a sense, what happened at the assembly of Latin American bishops in Medellín (1968) was that the church of the poor, of Las Casas, Beltrán, and Claver, captured the hierarchy, with the help and inspiration of the Second Vatican Council and Pope John XXIII. What is currently taking place in Latin American Roman Catholicism is a great struggle between that "new church," which is in truth old, and the understanding of the hierarchy and its function derived from the period of the royal *Patronato*.

Hispanic Catholics in the United States have had similar experiences. Until very recently, the hierarchy, even in those regions where most of the Catholic population was Hispanic, was non-Hispanic. While many of the priests, and certainly those who had closer contact with their parishioners, were Hispanic, they knew that the higher echelons of the hierarchy were closed to them. Thus Hispanic Roman Catholics have lived in a church that was sympathetic to their struggles at the local level but that usually ignored them at the national level. To them this was not new. It was rather a repetition of what had usually taken place under the Spanish regime, and then again under the various national governments in Spanish America.

63

At the local level, some priests followed the lead of the national hierarchy, while others sought ways, again at the very edge of obedience, to respond to the needs of their parishioners. Their task was not simply to preserve the religious traditions of their parishioners, although such traditions were important. Their task was rather to preserve their parishioners' right to exist as themselves, distinct not only from white Protestants but also from white Catholics. To exist, and to make a significant contribution both to society and to the church. To make a contribution, and to enjoy their just share.

What is happening in the Hispanic Roman Catholic Church in the United States is similar to what happened in the Latin American church at Medellín: This church of the poor is making itself heard. In recent years, a number of Hispanics have come to occupy positions of authority in the Church, as bishops or as directors of institutions and programs. When some of the present-day bishops were considering the priesthood, their friends tried to dissuade them, because they were Hispanic and there was no future in the Church for them. Now they are part of the hierarchy.[24] But some of them are a different sort of hierarchy. They are not the heirs of the bishops appointed by the crown but rather of the friars who struggled for justice for their people. In them, a new day is dawning in the Roman Catholic Church, and Catholic Hispanics are very much aware of this.

In 1969 the National Conference of Catholic Bishops established the Division for the Spanish Speaking. In 1970 its Director, Mr. Pablo Sedillo, was appointed. Since that time, the division—now the Secretariat for Hispanic Affairs of both the National Conference of Catholic Bishops and the United States Catholic Conference—has emphasized the need for grassroots involvement of Hispanics in planning for the mission of the Church. The Primer Encuentro Nacional Hispano de Pastoral took place in June of 1972, with approximately 250 participants. The Second Encuentro Nacional Hispano de Pastoral took place in 1977. By this time, however, a new methodology had been developed. In this methodology, the process leading to the Encuentro was at least as important as the Encuentro itself. As the planners stated,

> The process leading to the Second Encuentro should serve to take the historic step from a mass Church to a Church of small ecclesial communities. It would therefore be an occasion for intensifying the creation and the renewal of these small communities throughout the country.[25]

From the beginning, it was stipulated that no one would be allowed to participate in the Encuentro without prior involvement in one of these basic groups. It was also hoped that the result of the process, as well as of the Encuentro itself, would be that in these basic Christian Communities (Comunidades Eclesiales de Base, or CEBs) the conclusions of the Encuentro would take flesh—and perhaps even, as they put it, blood. The theme of the Encuentro was "Evangelization," understood in its widest sense, as implying a continuous process throughout life whereby believers are increasingly closer to Christ and to a full commitment to the gospel. This will result in sharing the message with others, both in word and deed, seeking the transformation of the world.[26]

The preparation for the Third Encuentro involved thousands of CEBs throughout the nation. At every level, flowing through parish, diocese, and CEB, there was ample consultation, study, and reflection. When the 1,150 delegates finally gathered in Washington in August of 1985, there was a growing consensus among Hispanic Catholics as to what their plan of ministry should be. Out of that Third Encuentro came the working document *Pueblo Hispano—Voz Profetica*, which would be used as the basis for preparing a National Pastoral Plan for Hispanic Ministry to be presented before the bishops in 1987.

The report of the Third Encuentro is a vast document covering various aspects of church life, and it is impossible to review it here. However, in order to understand the mood and the dreams of Hispanic Catholics, a few quotations may be in order:

> The Word of God gives us strength to denounce the injustices and abuses that we suffer; the marginalization and scorn, the discrimination and exploitation. It is in the Word of God that we, as pilgrim people, find the motivation for our daily Christian commitment.[27]

> . . . We call upon the Christian community (lay people, bishops, deacons, religious priests) to show the world that worldly things and human institutions, through the determination of God the Creator, are also ordered to the salvation of people, and therefore, may contribute to the building up of the body of Christ. That is why as Christians we have the responsibility to work for social justice.[28]

> . . . We also announce a model of Church that is open to the people's needs, placing its buildings at the disposal of the people and recognizing the reality of Hispanics as a poor community. We affirm a model of priesthood that is more in contact with the people it serves, dedicated to persons, not material buildings, and exercising leadership in smaller communities.[29]

The consequence of all this is that there are in the Catholic Hispanic tradition, both in the United States and in Latin America, many who are ready for the end of the Constantinian era. In Latin America, the

65

church of the poor, which has existed through the ages alongside the coopted church of the powerful, continues to live at the edge of obedience, lacking support from sociopolitical structures and usually opposed by them, even to the point of persecution and martyrdom. When the last vestiges of the Constantinian era finally disappear, this church will be ready for the new day, for it is already living in it. In the United States, Hispanic Catholics have learned how to subsist and to worship without the support of either the dominant white Protestant culture or the also dominant white Catholic subculture. As the post-Constantinian era advances, Hispanic Catholics represent that segment of the church which is best prepared to face the new day.

The Protestant Experience

Although all Hispanic-Americans have a Roman Catholic background, many of us are now Protestant. This growing Protestant Hispanic community has two origins, for some were converted in this country, while others were already Protestant at the time of their immigration. Therefore, to understand the Protestant Hispanic community in the United States, it is necessary to look both at Latin America and at this country.

When I look at Protestantism, both in Latin America and among Hispanics in the United States, I am once again surprised (although I am not as surprised by outward events as at myself) at what has happened to me and my views. As I was growing up, and my classmates were crossing themselves upon learning that we were Protestant heretics, my Protestant friends and I drew courage from a book that was quite popular among Latin American Protestants in those days. It was written by an Alsatian Protestant, Frédéric Hoffet, and its title was *Protestant Imperialism*.[30] The main thesis of the book was that Protestantism was conducive to higher culture and better living standards. It compared Protestant and Catholic countries on everything from literacy to illegitimate birth rates. It pointed to the superior technology of Protestant nations. It listed all the social evils and political unrest of Catholic countries. The conclusion, at least at that time, appeared irrefutable: Protestantism was destined to rule the future. Let my classmates cross themselves. We had a clearer vision of the future, a higher hope for our country and our society. And that vision and that hope were being realized at that very moment in the most advanced and progressive countries of the world.

This created a tension or an ambivalence in our view of culture and the society around us. On the one hand, we were profoundly counter-cultural. In order to be a Protestant in Latin America in those days, one had to have a strong Anabaptist streak. "No smoking, no drinking, no dancing" were not mere legalistic prohibitions. They were constant reminders that life around us was corrupt, and that we belonged to a different reality. Eschatology was very real, not always in the sense of an imminent expectation but rather in the sense that our hope was for a different city.

On the other hand, we were not always clear whether that city was made by human hands or not. As Hoffet seemed to indicate, the holy city was already being built elsewhere, in countries whose religious stance was the same as ours. In short, our countercultural stance was both eschatological and extraterritorial. We judged our society both by the yardstick of the Reign of God and by the yardstick of the North Atlantic.

In the early years of Protestant Christianity in Latin America, this ambiguity did not immediately lead to contradiction. Protestantism entered Latin America as a liberating force. The first Protestant missionary to Latin America, James Thomson, came as the representative both of a new method of public education and of the British and Foreign Bible Society.[31] Almost immediately after political liberation from Spain, Thomson traveled throughout the continent and the Caribbean, announcing intellectual liberation from ignorance and from the obscurantism of the Catholic Church and the Inquisition. As such, he was received joyfully by the political liberators of the continent, Bernardo O'Higgins, José de San Martín, and Simón Bolívar. After all, these early political leaders shared the view that in order to make Latin America truly free, ideals, principles, and even people must be brought in from the North Atlantic.[32] Placing the Bible in the hands of the people and inviting them to examine it freely was a revolutionary act. Protestant worship, where people participated actively, was also an act of empowerment and liberation. The same could be said for the polity of most Protestant churches—and I still remember how I gloated, telling my Catholic schoolmates about my right to vote on matters affecting the life of the church.

Missionary work, however, was only one of the sources of Latin American Protestantism in the nineteenth century. Another source—most important numerically in the southern tip of the continent, in Argentina, Uruguay, Brazil, and Chile—was immigration. Convinced as they were that democracy could only flourish with a people trained for it, the early leaders of these countries—probably not untainted by racist considerations—encouraged immigration from northern Europe. Such immigrants required religious freedom, which had not always been part of the original program of the wars of independence. Once this was granted to the immigrants, it became untenable to deny similar rights to native citizens. Soon, contact between the two communities produced increasing numbers of native Protestants.[33] Also, as the descendants of the immigrants became enculturated and many of them retained the faith of their ancestors, there developed a large Protestant community that was increasingly native.

In other cases, Protestant communities in Latin America grew out of natives who had been in exile in the United States, or who in some other way had been in touch with Protestantism. This was particularly true of Cuba, whose early Protestant communities were the result of missions sent by Cuban exiles in Florida.[34] These exiles had settled mostly in Key West and Tampa, and there many of them had become Protestant. By the third quarter of the nineteenth century, they had their own Cuban pastors, educated in seminaries in the United States. Since at that time the Spanish government was going through a relatively liberal period, some of these communities sent missionaries to Cuba. Others returned from exile and founded churches that later sought connection with one of the major Protestant denominations in the United States. After 1898 the number of returning exiles grew. Among them were a number of pastors, who became the first leaders of the emerging Protestant churches. When the first missionaries were officially sent by the churches in the United States, they found that much of the preliminary work had been done. Meanwhile, in Puerto Rico, in the town of Aguadilla, a community of "believers in the Word" had been founded by a traveler who had obtained a Bible in the Virgin Islands. This community eventually joined the Presbyterian Church.

Finally, a small number of Protestants in Latin America were the result of schisms within the Roman Catholic Church. In Mexico, President Benito Juárez clashed repeatedly with the Roman Catholic hierarchy, which he considered too aristocratic and retrograde. At that time, several priests left the Catholic Church, taking their flocks with them. Juárez himself used to attend services at one of these congregations. Eventually, these congregations joined the Episcopal Church.[35]

The ambivalence of early Protestantism in Latin America also created a duality in our ecclesiology. For all kinds of reasons, and with some exceptions, Latin American Protestantism was in its origins, and to a great extent still is, a church of the poor. It excelled in the education of poor children, in work among peasants, in providing medical assistance in the most forlorn places, in promoting literacy, and most especially in bringing the good news as we understood it to those who seldom heard any good news.

At the same time, however, it was a church whose ideal was so molded by the image of the North Atlantic that it could not really be a church of the poor. Its ideal was the middle-class church in the United States, from which it received so much economic support. The ideology that was thus associated with early Protestantism was that of the nineteenth-century bourgeoisie: education as the means to solve all national problems, government in the hands of the educated, freedom of thought and worship, free enterprise, and the rewards of personal effort. It was thought that the reason for the "backwardness" of our countries was that these ideas, and the education that went with them, were not sufficiently widespread, and that we still carried the ballast of centuries of obscurantism and Catholic authoritarianism. If we could only rid ourselves of that inheritance, our countries would join those of the North Atlantic in their economic and human progress. The poor were temporarily such, until they could become middle class, largely through the agency of the church and through improvement in their moral standards. If poor peasants were simply given education, healthy bodies, and some technical know-how, most of their problems would be solved. With such resources, hard work and clean living was the formula for success. The result was that there are now in every city in Latin America dozens of professionals, business people, and church leaders who were born in conditions of abject poverty and who owe their success to the church. But this view of the reasons for our social problems also meant, at least implicitly, that lack of success was the result of sloth or vice. And therefore the result was also that many of those successful people whom I have just mentioned feel that if they managed to succeed, others could manage just as well.

This was—and to some extent still is—the ideology of the "historic" churches. Methodists, Presbyterians, Episcopalians, and others have made most of their inroads among the middle classes, and usually through education. Since this was a time of economic expansion, which required a trained middle class, Protestant schools and churches often served as means for social climbing—although normally only to the lower echelons of the middle class—and thus the ideology of progress through education and through Protestantism seemed to be confirmed by the thousands of Protestants who could witness to the success they had achieved.

The twentieth century saw the introduction into Latin America of a different sort of Protestantism. This was fundamentalism, whose birth as a self-conscious movement may be dated from the Niagara Falls declaration of 1895. In the early decades of the present century, the debate between fundamentalists and liberals raged in Latin America. By the middle of the century, there were numerous fundamentalist churches on that continent, and significant segments of the "historic" churches followed a similar orientation. This, however, led to very little change in the basic ideology of Latin American Protestantism. The most noticeable of these changes was in the devaluation of education, now suspected of leading to doubt as to the authority of Scripture. Freedom of thought, although discouraged in theological matters, was still theoretically encouraged. And there were few among the fundamentalists who doubted the principles of individual effort, free enterprise, and middle-class notions of success. Although often drawn from the lower classes, fundamentalist Protestants still thought in terms of middle-class goals and ideals.

Then came the enormous Pentecostal wave. The Azusa Street revival in Los Angeles began in 1906, and by 1910 the movement was so strong in Chile that a group of Methodists whose charismatic practices were condemned by the Annual Conference of Chile founded the Methodist Pentecostal Church. This denomination, which at first had only three congregations, soon outgrew its mother church and became one of the major Protestant denominations in Latin America. Similar events have taken place in other parts of the continent, so that by now the characteristic form of Latin American Protestantism is Pentecostalism.

Although its approach to Scripture is similar to that of the fundamentalists, Latin American Pentecostalism is very different from fundamentalism. The latter is rigid in its structure and leadership, most of which remains foreign. Indeed, among some fundamentalist missionaries one often encounters the unspoken and perhaps unconscious assumption that only American missionaries are capable of safeguarding the true faith, and that Latin American converts are not entirely trustworthy on that score. For that reason, although fundamentalist churches have grown, they have not achieved the incredible success of Pentecostalism. Pentecostals, on the other hand, offer a mixture of rigidity and flexibility. Their emphasis on the power and freedom of the Spirit makes all human practices and institutions provisional. Also, most of the older Pentecostal churches in Latin America are autochthonous, and not the result of Pentecostal missionary work from abroad. Many of those that are not autochthonous have become largely indigenized. Therefore, these older Pentecostal churches are freer to find their own way in Latin American culture and society.[36]

For these reasons it is very difficult to characterize Latin American Pentecostalism. While there is in it a measure of escapism, with faith directed mostly toward a spiritual afterlife, there is also a significant measure of earthiness that other Protestants often refuse to acknowledge. Their theology, with the minor changes required by their charismatic orientation, is the same as that which many fundamentalist missionaries taught: the literal inspiration of Scripture, the salvation of the soul through faith in Christ, and the need for lives of purity while one waits for life in heaven. Their ideology is still the same as that of most Latin American Protestantism, although their daily life and social circumstances do not fit that ideology. The majority of them are poor and have learned by experience that poverty is not simply the result of sloth, vice, or ignorance. What thus results is a vast community in transition, seeking its way as it moves forward, with the outcome still in doubt.[37]

In any case, the one common characteristic of most Latin American Protestantism until recent times has been its strongly anti-Catholic persuasion. Since the surrounding culture bears the Catholic imprint at all levels, this has resulted in an alienation from Latin American culture. In this alienation, Latin American Protestants have often looked to Protestant nations, and particularly to the United States, as paradigms of what they wish their own nations could become. Thus Protestant alienation in Latin America has usually been not only otherworldly but also foreign oriented.

One of the main sources of Hispanic Protestantism in the United States has been the migration of Latin American Protestants to this nation. This migration, often precipitated by political and economic considerations, was often inspired at a deeper level by the Protestant ideology itself. The experience of immigration to the United States as a Protestant has already been described in the first chapter, and it is not necessary to repeat here what was said there. Suffice it to say that many such immigrants, finding their hopes ill-founded, have begun to doubt the ideology behind those hopes and have thus become a source of self-criticism in North American Protestantism.

But not all Protestant Hispanics in the United States entered the country as Protestants. Many were converted in the United States, through processes similar to those that took place in Latin America. In the nineteenth century, Protestantism appeared to be as the vanguard of progress, while Roman Catholicism, especially under Pius IX, was going through its most authoritarian and reactionary period. After the Mexican-American War, the Roman Catholic hierarchy in the conquered territories was in the hands of the invaders, and generally in their service. Actually, the first Mexican-American bishop was not named until well into the second half of the twentieth century. These circumstances gave rise to anticlerical feelings similar to those which appeared in Latin America at the time of independence. And this in turn opened the way for Protestantism.

Also, the Mexican-American War—as well as the Spanish-American War, which led to the conquest of Puerto Rico—was defended on ideological grounds as partly a religious war against backward and antidemocratic Catholicism. After the conquest, that ideology was used to justify it, and some of the conquered, as is usually the case, came to believe it. Thus Protestantism and the United States were seen by some as the forces of liberation from obscurantism and medievalism. If one wished to be attuned to the future, one had better join these forces, which were proving irresistible and which in any case were seen as positive. Thus while most clung to Roman Catholicism—even to a Roman Catholicism under foreign leadership—as the means to preserve their dignity and authenticity, others saw in Protestantism a way into the future, and into full participation in the nation that they had now unwillingly joined.

This, however, was not all that attracted Hispanics to Protestantism. The great appeal of Protestantism was in Scripture itself, which the Catholic Church had taught us to respect but not to read. For many Hispanics, both in the United States and in Latin America, the experience of hearing the Word for the first time, of being able to study Scripture in new ways, was revolutionary and liberating. After this, they could no longer understand how anyone could remain tied to a church that either forbade or discouraged the reading of Scripture, and they made every conceivable effort to bring other Hispanics to the same realization.

What is happening today is that the seam that held our ambivalence together is tearing apart. The result is the emergence of a new way of being Protestant among Hispanic Americans. From our earlier countercultural and quasi-Anabaptist stance, this new form of being Protestant retains its ability to be sharply critical of the culture and society around it. The difference is that now it is also critical of that other society, that North Atlantic that Hoffet so praised, and that we now know to be part of this old order that is to pass. From the other pole of our earlier ambivalence, we retain the insight that, however imperfectly and however provisionally, Christian life and action in society must conform to Christian values and to the vision of the future for which we hope.

This is not to say that all Protestants feel this way. There are many who still cling to the earlier understanding and still believe that as a greater proportion of the population becomes Protestant, social ills will be automatically solved. Therefore, just as Catholicism and Protestantism are divided in Latin America, so are they among Hispanics in the United States, and along lines parallel to those that cause divisions in Latin America.

A New Ecumenism

Ever since it encountered Protestantism, the Hispanic community lived in religious tension. On the one hand, Catholics felt that Protestants were not only heretics, as the hierarchy told them, but also traitors to their people and their traditions. On the other, Protestants felt that Catholics were not only antibiblical heretics and idolaters but also relics of an age of obscurantism.

The last few decades, however, have seen very significant changes in this situation. The renewal of Roman Catholicism since the time of John XXIII and the Second Vatican Council has been nothing short of miraculous. Even very conservative Protestants have been forced to admit that on the premises of their own theology, they cannot discount what may happen in a church that has begun to read Scripture anew and has set out on a daring pilgrimage of renewed obedience. Emphasis on the role of the laity has also increased participation in the life of the church at the local level, thus giving Hispanics added input into Roman Catholicism. Eventually, the first Mexican-American bishop was consecrated. He and others have not been content with following the patterns set by the earlier white hierarchy, and with their blessing other Hispanic priests have been organizing communities for social action, inquiring into the possibility of a Hispanic theology and in general bringing to the Hispanic Catholic Church the *aggiornamento* that Pope John inspired.

Meanwhile, Hispanic Protestants have also been on pilgrimage. Besides their own experience of injustice and alienation, which contradicted the ideology they had associated with Protestantism, there were other events that opened their eyes to new realities. The civil rights movement was foremost among these. This was basically a struggle of Protestants against Protestants. In that struggle, white Protestantism did not always show itself to be the force for progress and freedom that we had been told it was. Indeed, a strange anomaly appeared: Those whites who were constantly quoting the Bible were also contradicting it in their daily lives, and those who seemed to discount the authority of Scripture often seemed to have a clearer understanding of the biblical demand for love and justice. This has made it very difficult for many in the Hispanic Protestant community to continue being fundamentalist in the traditional sense. The authority of Scripture is still held in high regard by that community. But there is also a growing awareness that there is a certain sort of fundamentalism that is grossly antibiblical. For this reason, many Protestants are seeking ways of interpreting Scripture that, while respecting the authority of the Bible, are different from what we were taught. The net result is that we find ourselves walking along the same path with Roman Catholics.

This new ecumenism has a practical and political side. The civil rights movement has its counterparts in the Hispanic community, and in those counterparts Catholics and Protestants have been drawn together. This is true of those involved in the unionization of farm laborers in California, in community organization in the barrios of San Antonio and Los Angeles, in the struggle for independence in Puerto Rico, and in the search for more political participation in New York and Chicago. In these struggles, Protestant and Catholic Hispanics march arm in arm and are thus learning to undo many of the prejudices that have divided them. It is true that many Hispanics, both Protestant and Catholic, do not participate in these struggles; but for those who do, out of the struggle itself a new ecumenism has been born.

Furthermore, this new ecumenism is not limited to issues of "life and work." It also includes what have traditionally been called matters of "faith and order." Indeed, it is our contention that there can be no division between life and work on the one hand and faith and order on the other, for as we work and live out the gospel we gain new insights into the meaning of our faith and the proper order for the church.

There is a new reformation already in progress. This reformation is arising, like that of the sixteenth century, in the periphery of Christendom—in the Third World and among minorities in the traditional centers of Christianity. The chapters that follow will seek to outline some of the doctrinal implications of that reformation.

CHAPTER 5

Reading the Bible in Spanish

To someone who was upset because his preacher substituted the Revised Standard Version for the "original" King James, I once replied that the Bible was originally written in Spanish, and that God then translated it into Hebrew and Greek because at that time no one knew Spanish—yet! Such tongue-in-cheek chauvinism, which may have served its function then, is not what I mean by "reading the Bible in Spanish." Nor do I mean the obvious, reading it in a Spanish translation. What I mean is much more than that: If it is true that we bring a particular perspective to history and to theology, then we must also bring a particular perspective to the interpretation of Scripture. And, once again, it may be that this perspective will prove useful not only to us but also to the church at large.

A Noninnocent History

A point at which this is true is the relationship between our noninnocent reading of our own history and the manner in which Scripture presents the history of the people of God, for this too is history beyond innocence.

Indeed, it would be difficult for anyone who reads the Bible carefully, going beyond the level of "Bible stories," to idealize its heroes. Abraham pretends that Sarah is his sister in order to save his own skin and allows Pharaoh to lie with her without even knowing that he is taking a married woman. Jacob is the trickster par excellence, who robs his brother of his inheritance and his father-in-law of his sheep.[1] The Israelites who move into Egypt are the descendants not only of Joseph but also of his brothers who sold him into slavery and then lied to their

75

father. At the time of the Exodus, Moses is not too eager to take up his calling, and the Israelites refuse to follow his lead, yearn for the flesh-pots of Egypt, complain about their monotonous diet of manna, and in general prove themselves to be fickle and faithless. When they arrive at the Promised Land, they hesitate, because the inhabitants of the land seem to them like giants and make them feel like grasshoppers.

The entire book of Judges is a cycle of apostasy, punishment, repentance, and redemption, only to return to renewed apostasy:

> Then the Lord raised up judges, who saved them out of the power of those who plundered them. And yet they did not listen to their judges; for they played the harlot after other gods and bowed down to them; they soon turned aside from the way in which their fathers had walked, who had obeyed the commandments of the Lord, and they did not do so. Whenever the Lord raised up judges for them, the Lord was with the judge, and he saved them from the hand of their enemies all the days of the judge; for the Lord was moved to pity by their groaning because of those who afflicted and oppressed them. But whenever the judge died, they turned back and behaved worse than their fathers. (Judges 2:16–19a)

Even the heroes of this book are not knights in shining armor. Gideon, after all his exploits, collects as a tribute the golden earrings of his followers, and with them makes an idol that even he and his family worship. His son then becomes a tyrant who, among other crimes, kills seventy of his brothers. And Samson, of whom in our childhood we were told beautiful stories of bravery, is a social climber and a wenching fool.

Then the kingdom is established, and here again the story is not unambiguous. From the very beginning, there were those who saw the establishment of the kingdom as an apostasy, for Israel was simply imitating the customs of her neighbors and thereby rejecting her only King, Yahweh. The first king is both a success and a failure, and his dynasty is discontinued. Then comes David, the great king who, how-ever, has one of his generals killed in order to take his wife, and who is not even aware of the enormity of his crime until Nathan points it out to him. Solomon asked God for wisdom and was able to build the Temple. But he used his power for his own glory, accumulating riches against the will of God and eventually falling into idolatry. Then the kingdom was divided and followed a checkered history, until both Samaria and Jerusalem fell. All the while, numerous prophets pointed out the many evils and injustices that the kings and others who held power condoned and even promoted. Thus the minority reports of the prophets came to occupy a larger part of Scripture than the chronicles of the kings. But even such chronicles did not spare the kings, for in

76

them we find the records of their achievements as well as of their failures and their crimes. Nor do the prophets escape unscathed, for they too are depicted as human beings with flaws and mixed motives.

The New Testament view of history is no more innocent. It opens with a genealogy to which we would do well to pay more attention. Look, for instance, at the women mentioned in it. The first is Tamar, out of whose incestuous union with Judah were born Perez and Zerah. Then comes Rahab, the harlot of Jericho who hid the Israelite spies and thus saved her life and her family. Ruth, the wife of Boaz, is a Gentile. "And David was the father of Solomon by the wife of Uriah." Finally, the last woman mentioned is Mary, to those who were "in the know" a woman chosen by God, but to the world at large—and to Joseph himself until he is brought in on the "secret"—the unwed mother of an illegitimate son. This is very different from the "innocent" genealogies so common among those who today wish to show that their privileges come from long-established rights, and who very carefully hide the skeletons in their genealogical closets.

The disciples and the early church fare no better. They are confused, and in the end all but one abandon their Teacher. Nor is this something that is completely overcome by the events of Pentecost, for the legends of the great deeds of the apostles, traveling throughout the world preaching the gospel, have very little basis in the New Testament—or in fact. Those of whom we know, particularly Peter, were about as confused after Pentecost as they were before, for the Holy Spirit kept surprising them with unexpected calls to obedience. And among the early believers were such people as Ananias and Sapphira, Simon Magus, the "saints" in Corinth, the Judaizers who invaded Paul's Galatian churches, and the lukewarm Laodiceans of the book of Revelation.

In short, biblical history is a history beyond innocence. Its only real heroes are the God of history and history itself, which somehow continues moving forward even in spite of the failure of its great protagonists. Since this is also the nature of Hispanic history, it may well be that on this score we have a hermeneutical advantage over those whose history is still at the level of guilty innocence, and who therefore must read Scripture in the same way in which they read their own history.

To those who think of their own history in terms of high ideals and purity, this may seem to detract from the power and inspiration of Scripture. This, however, is not the case with Hispanics. We know that we are born out of an act of violence of cosmic proportions in which our Spanish forefathers raped our Indian foremothers. We have no skel-

77

etons in our closet. Our skeletons are at the very heart of our history and our reality as a people. Therefore, we are comforted when we read the genealogy of Jesus and find there not only a Gentile like ourselves but also incest and what amounts to David's rape of Bathsheba. The Gospel writer did not hide the skeletons in Jesus' closet but listed them, so that we may know that the Savior has really come to be one of us—not just one of the high and the mighty, the aristocratic with impeccable blood lines, but one of *us*.

The Consequence of an Innocent Reading of Scripture

The alternative is a selective reading of Scripture, similar to the selective reading of American history to which I have already referred. Ben Franklin must be seen as an intellectual, a diplomat, and even an eccentric, but not as a man casting a greedy eye on Indian lands. Likewise, Jacob's cheating, his sons' near fratricide, the wavering of the Israelites, Gideon's apostasy, Samson's folly, David's murderous adultery, Solomon's combination of wisdom and folly, and all other similar events must either be ignored or treated as the unfortunate background for what still amounts to an innocent history.

Such idealization of history is much easier when we come to the New Testament. On the basis of that idealization, the early church is raised to the status of a perfect model for us. We thus wish we could "preach like Paul," when the truth is that Paul could on occasion preach his hearers to sleep! That the early church has a certain paradigmatic authority is not to be denied. But this does not have to be equated with guiltless perfection—which itself, paradoxically enough, would destroy the value of the paradigm for us.

The relative ease with which guiltless history can be read into the New Testament has lead to a disparagement of the Old Testament among those who still believe in innocent history. If our history is one of great, and almost sinless, heroes, it is difficult to claim that the messy history of the Old Testament is somehow a Word of God to us. From such a perspective, the most we can do is read the Old Testament at the level of "Bible stories." A book of "Bible stories" usually includes the story of David and Goliath, but not of David and Bathsheba; the story of Solomon's wisdom in threatening to divide the disputed baby, but not of Solomon's idolatry. This is a subtle way of disparaging the Old Testament, for it amounts to improving on it. We are afraid that the violent and otherwise questionable narratives of the Old Testament would pollute our children's minds, and therefore we pollute them with a truncated view that parallels the view of American history with which they are being raised.

Such "Bible stories" are not politically and socially neutral. They have an agenda, albeit one hidden from the children who read them, from we who buy and distribute them, and even from those who write them. The agenda is precisely to promote an innocent reading of history. The parallels between the "Bible stories" read in our Sunday schools and the "American stories" that pass for history in our daily schools are striking. In both cases, the great heroes are depicted as people of pure and unmixed motives, clear conscience, and undeviating righteousness. If such is the story of the great Bible heroes, and of the great American heroes, biblical faith and flag waving go hand in hand. And this history, as already noted, serves to justify the present order as the result of the great deeds of those past heroes.

Innocent history is a selective forgetfulness, used precisely to avoid the consequences of a more realistic memory. A striking example of this is found in John 8:31–33, where after Jesus speaks his famous words, "The truth will make you free," some of his listeners answer, "We are descendants of Abraham, and have never been in bondage to any one. How is it you say, 'You will be made free'?" Incredible selective forgetfulness, which allows them to remember that they are descendants of Abraham and to forget that between Abraham and themselves stand bondage in Egypt, exile in Babylon, and now servitude to Rome! Incredible, and innocent. Innocent, and guilty, for its function is to avoid listening to the radical Word Jesus is announcing, which would require unwelcome changes.

Responsible remembrance, on the other hand, leads to responsible action. A clear example is in the repeated injunctions to Israel: "You shall not wrong a stranger or oppress him, for you were strangers in the land of Egypt" (Exod. 22:21); "Love the sojourner therefore; for you were sojourners in the land of Egypt" (Deut. 10:19); and an even more radical consequence of that memory of pilgrimage, "The land shall not be sold in perpetuity, for the land is mine; for you are strangers and sojourners with me" (Lev. 25:23). For white North Americans to remember that they are immigrants and that the land is not theirs would lead to an attitude toward the original inhabitants of the land, and toward more recent immigrants, that the present order cannot bear. Forgetfulness is the easy way out, just as it was for the children of Abraham who refused to remember their bondage in Egypt.

Therefore, part of our responsibility as Hispanics, not only for our own sake but also for the sake of other minorities as well as for the sake of the dominant group, is constantly to remind that group of their immigrant beginnings, of the Indian massacres, of the rape of the land, of the war with Mexico, of riches drawn from slave labor, of neocolonial exploitation, and of any other guilty items that one may be inclined to forget in an innocent reading of history.

On the other hand, a noninnocent reading of Scripture must not be confused with a sophisticated reading. If it is true that God has "hidden these things from the wise and understanding and revealed them to babes" (Matt. 11:25; Luke 10:21), there must be a place for a naive—not simplistic, but naive—reading of Scripture. It is significant that while traditional North Atlantic theology has usually taken for granted that Moses' great work was the receiving of the Law at Sinai, the anonymous Afro-Americans who wrote the spirituals always knew that in the biblical tradition Moses' great work of salvation was leading the people out of bondage in Egypt—a point on which most modern scholars now agree with the spirituals. It is also significant that while there is much discussion in academic circles about the typological understanding of Scripture and the view of history implied in that understanding, Christian Base Communities both in Latin America and the United States have long been interpreting Scripture along typological lines, as a means of inserting themselves into that history.

What has taken place is that even though those of us who are engaged in academic pursuits may not like to admit it, our own interpretations have been tainted by social and economic interests, which we have then defended on the basis of "intellectual objectivity." As biblical scholar Norman K. Gottwald has put it,

> The massive datum is that biblical scholars of the last two centuries have been firmly located in the middle class and have synthesized their scholarly humanistic ideals with bourgeois capitalism and, furthermore, have done so with surprisingly little sense of the inherent tensions and contradictions in such a synthesis.[2]

The Word of God in the Older Testament

The disparagement of the Hebrew Scriptures has often been a temptation for Christians. Already in the second century, Marcion claimed that the Old Testament was the word of a different god who was not the Father of Jesus Christ. The god of the Old Testament, the creator god, is involved in this material and unhappy world, which he made either out of spite or out of ignorance and which he now rules on the basis of law and judgment. God the Father, on the other hand, is a God of grace and forgiveness, who rules in love and who promises salvation out of this evil and material world. The early church saw clearly that Marcion's doctrines were incompatible with many of its fundamental teachings, such as creation, the incarnation of Jesus Christ in true flesh, and the resurrection of the body. For this reason, it rejected his teachings—indeed, the core of our present Apostles' Creed was composed in order to make clear that those who held to apostolic faith rejected Marcion's views.[3]

Yet Marcionism, in disguised and somewhat mitigated forms, has been a constant temptation for Christians. The way it is most often heard in our churches and Sunday schools is the notion—which is historically false—that the Old Testament speaks of God as lawgiver and judge, whereas Jesus' great contribution was to speak of the love of God, and to call God "Father."

A slightly more sophisticated semi-Marcionism is even more prevalent and stands at the root of the "Bible stories" to which I have already referred. This semi-Marcionism holds that since Jesus is the final and supreme revelation of God, the whole of Scripture is to be read and interpreted from the viewpoint of his message. This is true as far as it goes. But it forgets that since the Old Testament is the history of God's revelation and action in preparation for the coming of Christ, the message of Jesus must also be interpreted in the light of that revelation and action. In other words, the argument of the new semi-Marcionites fails in that it takes for granted that without the preparation of the Old Testament, we know what Jesus' message is. History shows that this is not true, for in the early church, as increasing numbers of Gentiles began to join the Christian community, it was clear that these Gentiles needed the background of the Old Testament in order to understand what the message was all about. Otherwise, they risked viewing Christianity as the gnostics and Marcion did. It was for this reason that Christian leaders insisted on the authority of the Old Testament.

Today, there is no guarantee that, in the midst of a society that is all the more pagan because it no longer even sees the radical difference between paganism and biblical faith, we can understand the message of Jesus any better than could the early Gentile converts. For that reason, while it is true that we are to interpret the Old Testament in the light of God's revelation in Jesus, it is also true that we are to understand the latter in light of the Old Testament.

It is in order to signify this that I prefer to refer to the Hebrew Scriptures as the "Older" Testament. In our common usage, the word "old" has the connotation of "obsolete," and therefore the term "Old Testament," particularly in contrast to the "New" Testament, tends to support our present semi-Marcionite heresy.[4]

If the Older Testament too is the Word of God, it follows that we cannot understand the Newer Testament in such a way that it appears that the Older Testament is on the whole unrelated to the Newer, or that one supersedes the other. And yet that is precisely what we have done in many and subtle ways. For instance, in the Common Lectionary used by most major denominations in the United States, during the Easter season readings from the book of Acts are substituted for the readings from the Hebrew Scriptures. Whatever the reasons may be for such an arrangement, part of the—perhaps unintended—message implicit in this practice is that after the resurrection of our Lord we no longer need the Older Testament—or in any case that we as the church are part of a new history with little or no connection with the history of Israel. (A further consequence of this use of the Lectionary is that we read the book of Acts "backwards," as it were, reading the history of the church as leading to Pentecost!)

Likewise, the Lectionary includes readings from the prophets only in reference to the Christian calendar, leaving out most of their harshest calls for social righteousness. The result is twofold: First, the message of the prophets is truncated, for their role is now limited to that of announcers of the coming Messiah, and little is said of their message to their own age and people. Second, the role of Jesus is also truncated, for he is now limited to being a "spiritual" savior and is understood apart from the great prophetic tradition of which he is part and culmination.

On the basis of this veiled disparagement of the Older Testament, it is quite possible to understand "spirituality" in terms of detachment from the world and its political realities. Yet it is clear that most of the Older Testament is dealing precisely with such realities. To this I shall return in another chapter, when I deal with what I term "political spirituality." For the time being, let it suffice to raise the question of how is it possible for what we usually call "spirituality" to be central to the Bible and yet almost unheard of in the Older Testament. Such a question should prompt us to inquire further as to the nature of biblical spirituality.

A similar and not unrelated case has to do with the doctrine of redemption. There is no doubt that one of the central themes of Scripture is redemption. But what we have been taught to understand by "redemption" and by "salvation" is hardly to be found in the Older Testament, if at all. If life after death is indeed the central message of Scripture, isn't it odd that in most of the Older Testament it is not even mentioned, and that Christians have to hunt carefully in order to find what might be a reference to it in the book of Job or in the Psalms? This is not to say that the Bible is not concerned with life after death, nor that such life is not a fundamental aspect of Christian hope. It is to say that no matter how true the promise of such life is, that promise is not the central thrust of Scripture.

Were it not for the presence of the Older Testament, we could be content with the commonly held notion that the good news of Jesus is that there is life after death and that this life is available through him. It is true that the New Testament affirms that there is life after death. But this was well known by the Pharisees long before the advent of Jesus and therefore would hardly be "good news" to them. The core of the good news is that the resurrection has already begun in the raising of Jesus from the dead. This certainly means that we can trust in him for our final resurrection. But even more, it means that the long-awaited promises have now begun to be fulfilled. The Reign of God has dawned. Life after death is good news. But it is not *all* the good news, for the Older Testament reminds us that the scope of God's action and revelation includes much more than life after death. The witness of the Older Testament reminds us that God's salvation is not purely "spiritual," in the common sense of that term, but is also political and social.

The Political Agenda

The understanding of the Bible as a book that deals essentially with "spiritual salvation" after death can be proven to be the result of the introduction of Christianity into the Greco-Roman world, with its preconceived notions of the nature of religion. But this is more than a historical accident, for it also carries with it a political agenda. That political agenda, simply put, is to make God apolitical. If God is primarily interested in the salvation of souls, and not in bodies and in how we distribute the things necessary for physical life, God is not interested in politics—for politics is, after all, the process whereby a society decides how its material resources are to be allocated. And if God is apolitical, it follows that believers ought to be equally apolitical, or at least that they ought not to mix faith and politics.

The problem is that if it is true that human beings are political animals, then everything that we do has a political context and political consequences. Thus the "apolitical" Christianity that many advocate is in truth a Christianity that supports the politics that exist, that is, the power of those who are presently powerful. What is usually meant by "mixing politics and religion" is very selective, depending on what kind of politics is actually being mixed with religion. To pray at the U.S. Congress, to preach in the White House, or to "give the blessing" at a stockholders' meeting is not political and is therefore acceptable. But to speak at a farm workers' rally, to bless their efforts to organize, or to criticize the Immigration Service is political. To attend a prayer breakfast with the governor of Puerto Rico is not political. To protest the presence of the Navy in Vieques is political. If one looks at the clear contradictions in such views, it is clear that the "apolitical" understanding of Christianity is very political indeed and is intended to support the agenda of the status quo.

Therefore, the modern semi-Marcionite heresy is not just a theological error or some innocent misconception we were taught in Sunday school. It is the ideological arm of political conservatism. To this conservatism, it is important that the Older Testament be set aside, for it speaks too much of a God who demands justice in human dealings, and part of whose redemptive work has to do with the establishment of such justice.

These political conservatives can draw on the New Testament as the basis for their supposedly "apolitical" brand of Christianity, simply because the entire New Testament was written during a period when the people of God had little or no power, and therefore the ordering of society was not an agenda on which they could have an immediate or direct impact. The Older Testament, dealing as it does with centuries in the history of the people of God, deals with various political situations and shows more concern for them than is shown in the New Testament. In any case, when we read the New Testament through the preparation provided by the Older, we find that its view of the purposes of God is not as purely "spiritual" as we are told it is by "apolitical" Christians.

What we then need is a new reading of Scripture, "in Spanish," so to say. Since the time of the Reformation, and particularly in Protestant circles thereafter, great emphasis has been placed on making the Bible available in the vernacular. We have usually thought that the significance of this was simply that people could now read for themselves what previously was reserved for scholars. But perhaps we ought to see another dimension in what happens when the Bible is read in the vernacular. It becomes the people's book, no longer under the control of those who control society. When the people read the Bible, and read it from their own perspective rather than from the perspective of the powerful, the Bible becomes a mighty political book. This is what I mean by "reading the Bible in Spanish": a reading that includes the realization that the Bible is a political book; a reading in the "vernacular," not only in the cultural, linguistic sense but also in the sociopolitical sense. In the high Andes, the equivalent of our reading in Spanish would be a reading in Quechua, and from the perspective of the Quechua-speaking peoples oppressed by the Spanish-speaking.[5]

The Grammar of This New Reading

In another book, my wife and I have suggested some guidelines or procedures for this new reading.[6] Without repeating what was said there, the following outline of a "grammar" for reading the Bible "in Spanish" may be useful:

1. To say that the Bible is a political book means, first of all, that it deals with issues of power and powerlessness. This is the fundamental political question, and it is also one of the central issues in Scripture. We must read our Bible again. Read it "in Spanish," that is, as exiles, as members of a powerless group, as those who are excluded from the "innocent" history of the dominant group, and we shall begin to see that it is indeed a political book. When we approach a text, we must ask first not the "spiritual" questions or the "doctrinal" questions—the Bible is not primarily a book about "spiritual" reality, except in its own sense, nor is it a book about doctrines—but the political questions: Who in this text is in power? Who is powerless? What is the nature of their relationship? Whose side does God take? In this approach to Scripture lies the beginning of a Hispanic-American theology, as well as the heart of the new reformation of the twentieth century.

2. We must remember that only a small portion of Scripture was originally written to be read in private. Spanish, like Greek and Hebrew, distinguishes between the singular and plural forms of the second person. The singular "you" as a form of address to the reader appears rarely in Scripture—the most notable exceptions are Philemon, I and II Timothy, and Titus.[7] Unfortunately, English no longer makes a distinction between the singular and the plural forms of "you." The old King James Version "ye" is no longer used. Therefore, when we read a biblical injunction addressed to "you," particularly when reading the Bible in private, we tend to think of each of us as an individual, and not of all of us as a community. This leads to the privatization of faith and its demands. In order to avoid this, the "grammar" for a new reading of Scripture "in Spanish," so to speak, must be aware that even when we read Scripture in private, God is addressing all of us as a community of faith.

3. We must remember that the core principle of scriptural "grammar" is its availability to children, to the simple, to the poor. Jesus rejoices "that thou hast hidden these things from the wise and under-

standing and revealed them to babes." To read the Bible "in Spanish" means to give attention to what the "babes" find in it. This may not be as sophisticated as what we find in our commentaries. It probably will not be as "religious" nor as "inspiring." But it may well be truer to the message of Scripture. Thus the ABCs of this grammar are to be found in providing opportunity for those who do not usually form part of our Bible study groups to read Scripture and tell us what it says to them in their situation.

4. Above all, however, we must learn to read Scripture in the vocative. The purpose of our common study of Scripture is not so much to interpret it as to allow it to interpret us and our situation. The interpretation of Scripture is important, for without it we run a greater risk of misunderstanding what is has to say to us and about us. But the final purpose of such interpretation is *not* to understand the Bible better. It is rather to understand *ourselves* better in the light of the Word of God, and to discover what obedience requires of us.

"Thy word is a lamp to my feet and a light to my path," says the Psalmist (119:105). Travelers who carry a lamp take care that it shines properly and that its lenses are clean; but if in the middle of their trek in the dark they become overly preoccupied with their lamp, looking at it instead of at the path, they will soon lose their way. The lamp is a means to an end, not an end in itself. To look at the lamp as if it were the path can only lead to disaster.

And yet this is what we have often done with Scripture. We do this at all levels. At a certain level, this is the fundamentalist error: to believe that the path is *in* Scripture, that to penetrate Scripture is to walk with God, that the Bible is its own end. But this is also the error of much biblical scholarship, which never returns from the written text to the context in which we must live today. If at the time of the Reformation Scripture was the captive of dogma and ecclesiastical authority, today it is often made the captive of historical criticism, textual analysis, form criticism, or whatever the latest word in biblical scholarship may be.

The problem with such practices is not in the scholarship. On the contrary, the scholarship is necessary so that we may come to a better understanding of the text itself, of its setting and its meaning in its time. The problem is rather that they often take the Bible away from its proper function, which is to lead the people of God in their historical pilgrimage, and never return to that function.

Reading the Bible "in the vocative" means reading it with the clear awareness that we are not before a dead text, for the text that we address addresses us in return. It is in this manner that the Bible is most often read in Hispanic communities. It is true that the influence of fundamentalism is still strong in Hispanic churches. It is also true that many leaders try to make use of the tradition of liberal biblical scholarship in order to break the stranglehold of fundamentalism. But when one participates in the life of the Hispanic church, one soon discovers that the Bible is most frequently read in a different manner, one that disconcerts both fundamentalists and liberals. The reason is that the Bible is read in the vocative, as the living Word of the living God, giving us not so much information about correct doctrine or about times past as direction as to who we are in our present time. In the Hispanic community, the biblical interpretation that is most appreciated is not the one that helps us understand difficult passages in the text but rather the one that helps us understand our own difficult passages in the pilgrimage of obedience. In the Hispanic community, when the Bible is read, there is the genuine expectation that we are about to learn something significant, not only about Moses or about Christian doctrine but also about ourselves and our world.

Needless to say, there is still much work to be done in our Hispanic churches as we seek to read Scripture with this grammar. There are many influences around us that try to compel us to read the Bible either as fundamentalists or as liberals—in either case, reading it as if it were an end in itself. We often succumb to such pressures. Yet in our better moments we are able to transcend both of those positions precisely because we read the Bible "in the vocative": because we read it seeking a reading of ourselves and our situation.

CHAPTER 6

Let the Dead Gods Bury Their Dead

Some years ago, a great hue and cry was raised—mostly by journalists—over the phrase "God is dead." Then the theology of the death of God, like its own god, languished and died. This was to be expected, for although these theologians made some very significant points, after the funeral of a loved one there is little for survivors to do but return home and attempt to build life anew.

The Limits of God-Talk

The crucial question, however, is not whether God exists, but who or what this God is whose existence we either affirm or deny. Some gods are better dead than alive. Humankind did not lose a great deal when Huitzilopochtli and his cohorts lost their power to require human sacrifices, or when the crocodiles of the Nile lost their divinity. The death of many gods has meant life for countless human beings. Therefore, let us not be too hasty in our condemnation of those who say that the "God" worshiped by much of our civilization is dead. Perhaps that "God" too is an idol whose day has passed. And perhaps biblical believers ought to rejoice at the funeral of such a god.

The question of the existence of God has meaning only insofar as we clarify what we mean by "God." Even then, it may well be that the nature of God is such that by definition such existence can never be proven but only accepted (or denied) by faith. Indeed, the so-called proofs of the existence of God involve from their very outset an implicit definition of what they are attempting to prove, and their conclusions can never go beyond the parameters set by those definitions. Thus, for instance, if we follow the "cosmological" proof, whose classic example is Thomas Aquinas' "five ways," and argue that everything that exists has a cause and that therefore there must be a first cause of all things, we have at best only proven the existence of a first cause, and not necessarily that of the God of Abraham. Likewise, even if Anselm's "ontological" argument had no logical flaws, and the very notion of "that-than-which-no-greater-can-be-thought" did necessarily include its existence, such an argument would only show that "that-than-which-no-greater-can-be-thought" does indeed exist; but it would still be necessary to show that "that-than-which-no-greater-can-be-thought" is identical with the God of Jesus Christ and the Ruler of the Church.

This leads us to an obvious conclusion: Any God whose existence can be proven is an idol. The difference between the God of Israel and the idols of the surrounding peoples is not that the latter are visible and God is not. When Scripture mocks and condemns idols made out of wood, what it ridicules and rejects is not the wood out of which they are made but the very fact that they are made by humans who then turn around and worship their own creations. In the second century, a Christian apologist, Aristides, saw this clearly when he said of the pagan gods, "Shutting them up in temples, they worship them, giving them the name of gods, and they carefully guard them so that thieves may not steal them, without realizing that a guardian is greater than that which is guarded, and that the one who makes a thing is greater than the thing."[1]

Any human creation that is raised to the level of the divine is an idol. This obviously includes all sorts of images of beasts and human beings made out of wood or metal. But it also includes intellectual images made out of ideas and lucubrations. Therefore, any proven god is an idol. Inasmuch as any proof can only prove that which its parameters allow, the shape of that which is proven has been defined previously and surreptitiously by the one offering the proof. Into this mold the notion of God is cast, just as the pagans of old cast their idols in the molds of smiths.

Nor is anthropomorphism the sign of idolatry, or of a "more primitive" understanding of God. In fact, all language about God must necessarily be anthropomorphic, inasmuch as it must be human language. We have no ultra-human categories with which to refer to God. It is not only when we speak of the "hands" of God that we are using anthropomorphic language. When we speak of the "will" of God, although no longer speaking as if God had a body, we are still within the bounds of anthropomorphism. We may attempt to overcome this difficulty by resorting to analogy and say therefore that God is "like" a father, emphasizing at once the similarities and the differences between God and human fathers.[2] Such language may be very helpful. But it does not free us of the charge of anthropomorphism, for only insofar as God is "like" a father does that assertion convey any meaning. Or we may seek to describe God by projecting that which we consider positive to the umpteenth power: God is *omni*potent, *omni*present, *omni*scient, and so on. But apart from the fact that we have no idea what we mean by "omni," what we are actually doing in such a case is simply exaggerating human characteristics that we consider desirable, and therefore we are still bound by anthropomorphism. Finally, we may follow the opposite tack and speak of God in purely negative terms: God is *im*passible, *in*finite, *un*created, and so on. But all that this means is that God is like nothing that we know—and to say that something or somebody is "like nothing" is hardly to say anything at all.

Anthropomorphic language should not scare us. We have no other language. We have no other categories. If there is a God who has chosen to reveal Godself to us, such revelation must come to us in terms and categories we can somehow grasp—that is, in human terms and categories. If there were a pitcher who could throw a baseball with such velocity that no one could catch it, such a pitcher would be a useless player. A divine revelation in purely divine terms would be no revelation at all. This in turn means that the fact that a theological statement uses anthropomorphic language is no valid reason for rejecting that statement—unless one is willing to abandon God-talk altogether. Failure to recognize this fact has produced—or at least supported—grave distortions in Christian theology, for Scripture certainly speaks of God in anthropomorphic terms, and theologians have often felt compelled to improve on the Bible as regards this point.

Acceptance of anthropomorphic language about God, however, is much more than a mere inconvenience to which we must submit, given the limitations of our mind and language. Beyond that general human reason for anthropomorphic language, there is a specifically Christian reason for the unashamed use of it: our central confession that God's supreme self-disclosure has come to us in a human being, Jesus of Nazareth. The incarnation must be the basis not only of our doctrine of redemption but also and above all of our doctrine of God. In another chapter we shall return to the doctrine of incarnation itself. But at this point it is necessary to note that the incarnation is not, as we often suppose, a last-minute remedy for human sin. It is much more than that. As second-century theologian Irenaeus would say, it is the very goal of creation.[3] And later, during the iconoclastic controversy, John of Damascus would hit the nail on the head by showing that some of the objections of the iconoclasts were based on a limited view of the significance of the incarnation for our understanding of God. Indeed, argued the Damascene, the objections of the iconoclasts are no longer valid once "God in His bowels of mercy became in truth man for our salvation, ... and after He lived upon the earth and dwelt among men, worked miracles, suffered, was crucified, rose again and was taken back to heaven."[4] The incarnation, in which God has become human, requires the rejection of any argument that God cannot be depicted in human terms. Whatever other reasons there may be for rejecting the use of icons, the argument based on the absolute transcendence of the divine has been refuted by God in the very act of incarnation.

Another reason why anthropomorphic language should not deter us is the doctrine of the *Imago Dei*—the image of God in human creatures. This doctrine, which early Christian theologians such as Irenaeus tied closely with the incarnation, affirms that we have been created after the divine image. If that is so, the use of anthropomorphic language is validated by the very fact that humans are "theomorphic." In other words, so-called anthropomorphic language about God is grounded in the presupposition not that God is like us but rather that we are like God.

How Does Scripture Speak of God?

Clearly, the Bible never attempts to speak of God in Godself. On the contrary, the Bible always speaks of God in relation to a creation and a people. God is not depicted in Scripture as "the prime unmoved mover," as "pure actuality," or as "absolutely simple." When the Bible speaks of God, it speaks of creation and redemption. When it refers to God's will, it does so in terms of a call to human obedience. When it speaks of God's "heart," it deals not with the inner workings of the Godhead but with God's purposes and feelings—yes, feelings, why not?—for humans.

Nowhere does the Bible say that God is impassible. On the contrary, there are repeated references to the divine anger, love, and even repentance! God walks in the garden. God wrestles with Jacob and haggles with Abraham. God is like a stern judge who will be moved by the impertinence of a widow. God is love. Thus if there is any sense in which the God of the Bible can be described as "immutable," this has nothing to do with impassibility or ontological immobility, but rather with the assurance that God's "steadfast love endureth forever."

Furthermore, the God of Scripture is an active participant in human history. God calls Abraham out of Ur and leads him in his wanderings. God breaks the bondage of Israel in Egypt. God smites tens of thousands of Israel's enemies. God raises judges to liberate Israel and punishes the nation for her iniquity. God sends prophets and conquerors to rebuke the people and their rulers. God takes human flesh. God promises a reign of justice and peace, a new Jerusalem where God will forever dwell with the people. In every one of these sentences, God is the subject. God is the active and sovereign ruler of history.

And yet, the God of the Bible is also the object, and even the victim, of history. God does not rule the world with an iron fist, as Pharaoh ruled over Egypt or Pinochet ruled Chile. God does not destroy all opposition with a bolt from heaven. Nor is opposition something God has created—like the military dictator who sets up an opposition party in order to claim that his rule is democratic. Although all things are created by God, God's free creatures have set up an empire of evil that denies and challenges the divine power. Evil is real and powerful. It cannot be dismissed or explained away as a necessary step in a great cosmic plan. God will indeed use it to achieve the divine goals, and perhaps those goals will so use evil itself that Christians who sing the traditional Easter Eve hymn are justified in saying, referring to the sin that has opened the way for redemption in Jesus Christ, "O blessed sin." But in spite of this, God does not will evil. God does not will injustice. Furthermore, inasmuch as God suffers with the oppressed, God suffers oppression and injustice. This fact, well attested throughout Scripture, finds its clearest expression in Jesus Christ, in whom God is carried to and fro by human beings whose victim God becomes. If being a minority means being subjected and victimized by forces one does not control, God is a minority!

Does this, then, deny the power of God? Certainly not. The Crucified is also the Risen One, who shall come again in glory to judge the quick and the dead. What it denies is an easy jump from creation to resurrection, with no cross. The cross, standing between creation and final consummation, is not an accident. It is not something that could just as well not have happened. It is, on the contrary, the supreme instance of the manner in which God's power operates. God's final victory does not ignore human suffering but takes it up and vindicates it. Ours is not a victorious, uncrucified God, victorious like an undefeated football team. Ours is the God who achieves victory through suffering, and liberation through oppression. Ours is a God who, having known oppression, shares with the oppressed in their suffering. And it is precisely by virtue of that divine sharing that the oppressed can also share in God's victory (Heb. 2:14–18).

Some may object that this denies God's omnipotence. But nowhere in Scripture do we find the claim that God is omnipotent in the sense of being able to do whatever strikes the divine fancy. Such a notion is the result of human speculation and is therefore characteristic of an idol. "Can God make a stone so big that even God cannot move it?" "Can God make a round square?" "Does God always do what is good, or is it more accurate to say that whatever God does is always good?" These and other questions, posed—sometimes seriously and sometimes face-tiously—by theologians and others in the past, show the senselessness of speaking of "omnipotence" in the sense that God can do any and all things. Perhaps God can. Perhaps God cannot. What is clear is that *we* cannot know whether God can or cannot. All that we know of God's power is that God is certainly able to do what has been done as well as what has been promised. To the question, What can God do? we can only answer, "What God has either done or promised to do."[5]

Does not the Creed speak of the "Father Almighty"? Yes indeed; but the term *pantokrator,* which is translated as "almighty," does not refer to some real or imagined power of God to do any and all things.[6] What it was intended to mean in the original text was that God's rule extends over all things, that there is nothing that falls beyond the scope of divine activity—and it is therefore more an assertion about the world, about the "panta" over which God rules, than it is an assertion about God. What the Creed asserts is that nothing is entirely alien to this "Parent All-Ruling."[7] The divine omnipotence is always understood in Scrip-ture—as well as in early Christian tradition—in relation to the world and the destinies of humankind. In fact, one could even make a strong case for the proposition that the *pantokrator* clause has been introduced into the Creed precisely to refute a view of God that attempted to speak of the divine power as something that could and ought to be known apart from the limits of creation. The doctrine that the Creed in its early form was rejecting was that of Marcion, who taught that the Christian Parent was far removed from the Creator of this world. According to Marcion, the Creator has so bungled in the act of creation that the supreme Parent must send Christ in order to save us from the Creator's world. Thus although Marcion spoke of the power of the Creator in relation to the world, he described the power of the Parent as being apart from the world. In consequence of all this, the world, the body, and history turned out to be evil. It was in response to these views that the Apostles' Creed, which originated in Rome in the middle of the second century, affirmed belief in "God the Parent All-ruling." All that we know is subject to the rule of God, even though evil is currently denying that rule. And it is senseless to speak of the power of God apart from the things we know.

The same is true of the divine "omnipresence." Scripture does speak of God's presence in every place:

> Whither shall I go from thy Spirit?
> Or whither shall I flee from thy presence?
> If I ascend to heaven, thou art there!
> If I make my bed in Sheol, thou art there!
> If I take the wings of the morning
> and dwell in the uttermost parts of the sea,
> even there thy hand shall lead me,
> and thy right hand shall hold me. (Ps. 139:7–10)

But this is not some sort of uniform pressure that God exerts over every place at the same time, like atmospheric pressure. Scripture does not say that God can be found equally wherever we please to look. The prophet of old did not find God in the fire or in the whirlwind. God spoke to the disciples in Jesus, and not directly in Pontius Pilate. The biblical view of omnipresence does not mean that there are no moments or places in which God is particularly present. It means rather that there is no place in which we cannot count on the presence of God—even if this presence, as the Psalmist is well aware, is one of judgment. The biblical omnipresence of God is different from the metaphysical notion that goes by the same name and whose consequence is denial of the dynamic particularity of divine action.

In the same vein, to speak of God's "infinity" as the Greek philosophers spoke of the infinity of being is scarcely helpful. Like "omnipotence," we have no idea what "infinity" might mean. Etymologically, we know that it means "endless." But our mind has no categories with which to conceive of such a thing, and therefore as a supposed description of the being of God the word "infinite" hardly says anything. Its only value lies in its use, not as a metaphysical description, but rather as a reminder that we need not fear that God's power, love, and care will come to an end. In other words, it is simply a less poetic and probably less precise way of saying that God has been our refuge "from generation to generation," that God's "steadfast love endures forever," or that God is the same "yesterday, today, and tomorrow."

All this can be summarized in one phrase Scripture uses to characterize God: "the living God." The idols of the nations are dead, for they have no power or freedom to act. The "prime unmoved mover" of the philosophers, the "impassible," "omnipotent," "infinite" God is no more alive than the idols—of which, in fact, it is one. Therefore, the "death" of such a God ought not to cause any chagrin but rather rejoicing among Christians who seek to ground their faith on the biblical witness.

The Idol's Origin and Function

It is a well known fact that the omnipotent, impassible god whom we have just called an idol resulted from the encounter between early Christians and the Greco-Roman world in which they were called to witness. Forced to give account of their faith in the One God, and often accused of atheism because they had no visible gods, Christians had recourse to what the earlier philosophical tradition had said regarding the Supreme Being. Against those who accused them of impiety, the witness of Socrates and Plato was a powerful argument. If the best minds of the Greek tradition had asserted that above and beyond all beings there was a Supreme Being, this put Christians in very respectable company and confounded their detractors. Furthermore, Socrates' death under an accusation of impiety and of corrupting the morals of youth showed that the doctrine of the One God had never been popular, and that the truly enlightened could expect persecution such as Christians were now suffering.

As an apologetic argument, therefore, Christians began building bridges between the Supreme Being of the philosophers and the God of their faith. In this, they could follow the example of earlier Jews who had taken a similar tack—particularly Philo of Alexandria. On the basis of this argument, and others like it, some among the intelligentsia were converted, and eventually Christianity was recognized as respectable doctrine.

The problem, however, is that such apologetic bridges tend to bear traffic in both directions. While the earlier Christian apologists saw at least some of the crucial differences between Christian doctrine and Greek philosophy, as time passed some—eventually most—Christian theologians came to the conclusion that Scripture is best interpreted in the light of Greek philosophy—more specifically, Platonic philosophy. Thus, for instance, Clement of Alexandria asserted that nothing "unworthy" ought to be affirmed of God.[8] What this meant, as is clear as we read on in Clement's writings, was that wherever the Bible spoke of God in "crude" terms—that is, in non-Platonic terms—such speech ought to be understood figuratively, as a vast allegory. In the last analysis, what this implied was that philosophical speech about God was more precise, and that biblical utterances regarding the Godhead were seen as allegorical references, intended mostly for the less cultured or intelligent—or, as some would even say, for "carnal" Christians. By the fourth century, when the Arian controversy broke out, practically all theologians agreed on this point and conceived of God as essentially immutable and impassible. Indeed, an argument could be made that the

Arian controversy was the result of the incompatibility between such a notion of God on the one hand, and the doctrine of incarnation on the other—a theme to which I shall return elsewhere.

That such is the origin of much of what we call the "traditional" attributes of God, few will doubt. What we often do not see is the connection between such a view of God and the vested interests of the ruling classes. Indeed, the philosophy Christians espoused in this development had appeared in the golden days of Athens, and the philosophers who had produced it prided themselves in that philosophy was "the occupation of the idle," and that they stood high above "the many" (*hoi poloi*). Athenian society, like many other democracies, based its wealth in the labor of some—among them a high number of slaves—while others lived in relative leisure. To say that philosophy is the occupation of the idle was therefore to say that it was the occupation of the leisurely, of those who did not need to work because the ordering of society was such that others did the work while they had the leisure to philosophize.

It is not surprising that such philosophers conceived of changelessness as the supreme perfection, without which nothing can really be said to *be* in the strict sense. This was not the result of purely rational considerations, as they claimed and sincerely believed. It was rather the result of the "rational" considerations of a reason molded by the leisurely social class in which it took shape. To that class, as to any privileged class, social change—particularly change involving discontinuity—was abhorrent. The static ideal of the social order, transmuted into metaphysics, thus resulted in the ideal of being as changeless perfection.

Naturally, this is not to say that the "idle" philosophers of ancient Greece set out to develop an ontology that would justify their personal privileges. Had that been the case, Socrates would never have been condemned to death, precisely by the privileged in Athens. The interests of a dominant social class work much more subtly, pervading the mentality of those who form part of it, and even of those who are subject to it, to such a point that those interests are eventually confused with pure rationality. Socrates was accused of impiety precisely because he laid bare the inner contradictions of Athenian society and the ideology on which it stood. But in spite of that, he, and most certainly his disciple Plato, remained exponents of much of what the Athenian aristocracy valued. It has often been remarked that Plato's understanding of the ideal state and its order was essentially aristocratic, although an aristocracy of the intellect rather than of wealth. What has not been remarked as often is that the same is true of his metaphysics.

Therefore, when Christians, in their eagerness to communicate their faith to the Greco-Roman world, began interpreting their God in Platonic terms, what they introduced into theology was not a sociopolitically neutral idea. What they introduced was an aristocratic idea of God, one which from that point on would serve to support the privilege of the higher classes by sacralizing changelessness as a divine characteristic. Yahweh, whose mighty arm intervened in history in behalf of the oppressed slaves in Egypt and of widows, orphans, and aliens was set aside in favor of the Supreme Being, the Impassible One, who saw neither the suffering of the children in exile nor the injustices of human societies, and who certainly did not intervene in behalf of the poor and the oppressed.

It would be possible to follow the entire history of Christianity to see how this God functioned in favor of the privileged precisely by condemning change and sacralizing the status quo. In the next chapter, I shall be trying to show how these issues are at stake in our understanding of the doctrine of the Trinity. For the time being, however, it should suffice to show how this God functions in today's world.

As these pages are being written, there is in the United States a movement that proclaims itself in favor of prayer in public schools. People involved in the same movement have done everything possible to thwart bilingual education in public schools—a bilingual education that in most cases is merely remedial, thus already giving the impression that Spanish and other non-English languages are a handicap to education. The campaign against bilingual education is in fact part of a much vaster campaign against all sorts of changes that would tend to erode the privileges of the dominant group—budgetary cuts in social programs, new immigration laws, nonenforcement of civil rights legislation, nonenforcement of antipollution laws, concentration of greater power in the military-industrial complex, and so on. Thus the same political tendency that shows a significant lack of regard for the demands for justice of the biblical God urges prayer in school. Why? Certainly not because such prayer will make us a more just society—that does not seem to be a main concern of those who campaign for prayer in schools. Rather, the function of prayer in school would be to sacralize the order of what are still segregated schools—and have become even more so in recent years. This "God" to whom prayer will be addressed will not be the defender of the alien and the poor but rather the defender of our borders against "aliens"—who in Scripture have God's protection—and of the dominant culture against the inroads of minorities. This "God" is not the God of Scripture. It is a pagan god, and just as much an idol as were Baal and his cohorts.

Take another example. If the essential attributes of God are omnipresence, omnipotence, and omniscience, it follows that the most "godlike" institutions of our time are the transnational corporations, for they more than any other approach the ideals of omnipotence, omnipresence, and omniscience. This may seem somewhat facetious in its absurdity. But it is true that a view of God as the Omnipotent, Omnipresent, and Omniscient One places a positive valuation on such characteristics, and thus justifies and encourages a quest for power that the Bible would characterize as sinful. A "God" whose power is similar to that of transnational corporations is not the God of Scripture. This is an idol of dominance. Just as earlier agricultural societies had gods of fertility, or as Pharaoh's power was justified by Osiris, so is dominance as a goal justified by this idol whom modern society calls "God." To such a "God," it is better that no prayers be addressed, either in our schools or—worse still—in our churches.

Idols have a socioeconomic function. That this function is often hidden under the guise of piety by those whose interests the idols preserve, would seem to be a fairly modern notion, drawn in part from the Marxist critique of ideologies. But the truth is that this critique of idolatry is already found in Scripture. In Acts 19:24, for instance, we read of the connection between the worship of Artemis in Ephesus and the vested interests of the silversmiths whose trade depended on that worship. There we are told of "a man named Demetrius, a silversmith, who made silver shrines of Artemis," who "brought no little business to the craftsmen." Having called together these craftsmen, as well as others in related trades, he made a very illuminating speech:

> Men, you know that from this business we have our wealth. And you see and hear that not only at Ephesus but almost throughout all Asia this Paul has persuaded and turned away a considerable company of people, saying that gods made with hands are not gods. And there is danger not only that this trade of ours may come into disrepute but also that the temple of the great goddess Artemis may count for nothing, and that she may even be deposed from her magnificence, she whom all Asia and the world worship. (Acts 19:25–27)

The result of this speech was as Demetrius intended, for "when they heard this they were enraged, and cried out, 'Great is Artemis of the Ephesians!' "

What is significant in this entire episode is the manner in which Demetrius links the interests of his hearers—and indeed of the entire city of Ephesus, which profited from the worship of Artemis—with piety. His concern is based on both economic and religious considerations.

But the final result is an outburst of religious indignation, so that it appears that the only reason why the Ephesian crowd opposes Paul's preaching is that their religion has been attacked. It would have been difficult to start a riot with people crying, "Paul is threatening our business." But that is in effect the motivation behind the seemingly more religious cry, "Great is Artemis of the Ephesians!" Idolatry is used to serve the interests of those who profit from it.

The same is true in our day. The "God" who passes for the biblical God is used to protect the interests of North American investments overseas. That is the reason why so many people are incensed when they hear that Christians in the Third World are opposed to such interests, which to them is like opposing God. The idol, joined with the military-industrial-academic complex, supports the building of bigger and more devastating bombs, all in the name of the survival of Western civilization, which has come to be equated with Christianity. Like Demetrius of old, those who protect the vested interests of the privileged call us to be more "religious." But the truth is that they are calling us to the idol that supports the status quo. To such calls we should reply, "Let the dead gods bury their dead." Let the "God" of the privileged follow the path of Artemis, Huitzilopochtli, and the crocodiles of the Nile.

100

CHAPTER 7

The One Who Lives as Three

One of my professors at Yale used to say that he could make no sense of the doctrine of the Trinity. But he would then add that he was enough of a traditionalist to be bothered by his inability to see any significance in a doctrine that the church had always declared to be at the center of its faith. This, I suspect, is the attitude of many Christians who belong to churches that affirm Trinitarian doctrine, and who are willing to use Trinitarian formulae in their worship but who would be hard pressed to explain why this doctrine is significant, or what it means. Those of us who have felt that way are not alone, for during the last two centuries Trinitarian doctrine has played only a minor role in most theological work, be it fundamentalist, liberal, or Roman Catholic. Indeed, this has been true to such an extent that Karl Barth's opening of his *Kirchliche Dogmatik* with a discussion of the Trinity may be said to be an anomaly—one for which Barth himself finds precedent only by going back seven hundred years to Peter Lombard's *Sentences* and Bonaventure's *Breviloquium.*[1] And yet, like my professor some thirty years ago, most of us realize that the doctrine of the Trinity is somehow related to the core of the Christian faith and are hesitant to depart from it on the sole grounds that we can make no sense of it.

For these reasons, it may be well to look again at this ancient doctrine, for there is always a possibility that when we look at it from a Hispanic perspective—that is, from a perspective different from that of the dominant culture—we shall find in it dimensions that we had not suspected.

Trinitarian Doctrine and the Council of Nicea

It is clear that a great deal of our difficulty with the doctrine of the Trinity comes from our uneasiness with the language employed at Nicea and in subsequent formulations of the doctrine. Words such as *homoousios,* "hypostasis," "substance," and the like, are not part of our daily vocabulary, for they are entirely foreign to our usual way of thinking. Furthermore, they are just as foreign to Scripture and to its way of speaking about God. When this is taken into account, we seem to be justified in declaring that the Council of Nicea, in casting the doctrine of God in such terms, departed so radically from the biblical witness that we would do better to ignore its decisions, and to forgo all Trinitarian theology.

The matter, however, is not so simple, for while such terms as *homoousios* and "hypostasis" do not appear in Scripture, there is in the New Testament ample evidence that the church confessed faith in the Three long before the debates leading to the Council of Nicea. The Trinitarian baptismal formula in Matthew 28:19 is probably of relatively late origin. And the text often adduced from I John 5:7 is clearly a later interpolation: "Three bear witness in heaven: the Father, the Word, and the Holy Spirit; and these three are one." But the much earlier epistles of Paul show that from a very early time the Christian church held to faith in three, who in Paul are usually called God (or God our Father), the Lord Jesus Christ, and the Holy Spirit. Read, for instance, the opening words of what is probably Paul's earliest epistle, and therefore the earliest writing of the New Testament, I Thessalonians 1:2–5: "We give thanks to *God* . . . remembering before *our God and Father* your work ... in *our Lord Jesus Christ.* For we know ... that . . . our gospel came to you . . . in power and in the *Holy Spirit.*" Similar utterances appear throughout the epistles of Paul, several other writings of the New Testament (including I John 5, which remains a Trinitarian text even after the interpolation mentioned above has been deleted), and in early Christian documents outside the New Testament.

These early formulations are highly inconsistent, for some documents simply speak of the Three without further explanation,[2] while others seem to understand the matter in terms of the common angelological speculation of the time,[3] and still another speaks of the Word and the Spirit as the "hands" of God.[4] But the very variety of formulations, all relating to the same triad of Father (or God), Son (or Word or Lord), and Holy Spirit (or Spirit of God), in itself witnesses to a common faith, not yet articulated in a standard formula.

The same is true of baptism in the threefold name. It is true that in the book of Acts there are references to a "baptism in the name of Jesus" (Acts 8:16). But even there such baptism is considered defective, and where it had taken place the apostles laid their hands on the baptized so that they might receive the Holy Spirit. Thus the faith of the early church was not only in God, nor only in God (or the Father) and in the Lord Jesus, but also in the Holy Spirit. For that reason, apart from the events told in the book of Acts, baptism in the early church was usually in the threefold Name. This is reflected to this day in the threefold structure of most of our creeds, which are derived from questions posed to converts at their baptism. By posing those questions, the church sought to ensure that the newly baptized did indeed believe, as the ancient baptismal creed of Rome said, "in God the Father All-ruling . . . in His Son Jesus Christ . . . and in the Holy Spirit."

For these reasons, we must distinguish between faith in the God with a threefold Name and later formulations such as those promulgated at Nicea. No matter how misguided the bishops gathered at Nicea may have been, or how difficult their task may have been made by the manner in which the issues were posed, they were trying to articulate what had been the faith of the church for centuries.

The manner in which the issues were posed, however, was derived from the developments in the doctrine of God discussed in the preceding chapter. The doctrine of the absolute immutability of God led necessarily to the question of how such a God can relate to a mutable world. In a way, this was not a new problem, for already Plato had had difficulties in relating his world of ideas to the present world of transitory existence. The theory of "participation" he developed was an attempt, although not quite successful, to bridge that gap. At a later time, those who sought to employ Platonism to interpret the Judeo-Christian tradition had similar difficulties. The clearest case is probably Justin Martyr, the second-century apologist whose work did so much to bring together Christian doctrine and Greek philosophy. Justin, like Plato before him, began with the notion that perfection requires immutability and thus agreed that the Supreme Being, God, must be immutable. How, then, does that immutable God relate to this mutable world? Justin found his answer by drawing on the doctrine of the "logos," of ancient lineage among Greek philosophers. The logos then becomes the link between God and the world, between the mutable and the immutable. This was the basic framework within which Arianism, and much of the theology that refuted it, developed.

However, before we continue discussing the development of Tri-nitarian theology, it may be well to open a parenthesis to look at the other function the doctrine of the logos performed in Justin's thought: serving as a bridge between Christian revelation and classical philosophy. Indeed, in that philosophical tradition it had often been asserted that the world is understandable because it and the human mind both participate of the same common reason or "logos." In this context, the "logos" became the source of all true knowledge, and thus it could be said that all that anyone knew was known because of the logos. Joining this with the prologue to the Fourth Gospel, which speaks of the logos or "Word" of God becoming incarnate in Jesus, Justin argued that all that the great philosophers of antiquity knew, they knew because of the One who had become incarnate in Jesus. This in turn allowed him to make the astonishing claim that, in a sense, Plato and Socrates were Christians—although he hastened to explain that they knew the logos only "in part," whereas Christians who have seen Jesus have seen the "entire logos."[5]

The doctrine of the logos thus made it possible for Christians to incorporate whatever seemed "best" from classical culture, without thus denying the centrality of the incarnation of God in Jesus Christ. Therefore, this understanding of the logos was the basic justification for the process discussed in the last chapter, whereby the God of Abraham was assimilated to the impassible Supreme Being of the philosophers.

What is interesting from our standpoint, however, is that post-Constantinian Christianity seems to have had recourse to this doctrine only when those whom it was attempting to missionize could not be conquered by force of arms. To what extent this is true is a historical inquiry that should be undertaken at a future time. But it seems clear that the contrast between the missionary methods of Ricci in China and de Nobili in India on the one hand[6] and those followed in Africa and in Latin America by most missionaries on the other, were dictated by the pragmatic reality that the colonial empires supporting such missions could conquer Africa or Latin America, but not China or India. The result was the notion that the Chinese, for instance, showed signs of having been instructed by the logos, but that the same was not true of Africans or of American Indians. And from this it was a short step to the declaration that the Chinese were human, for the universal logos had spoken to them, but that the same was not true of the "savages" of Africa and the New World. These, showing no signs of the logos, were inferior beings, who did not truly own their land and who could be legitimately dispossessed and enslaved.[7]

Closing this parenthesis on the manner in which the doctrine of the logos has functioned in missionary and colonial expansion, we return to its place in the development of the doctrine of the Trinity. The problems that would later appear in Arianism were already present in Justin's theology, for they are derived from the same framework in which the difference between God and the world is seen in terms of the contrast between mutability and immutability. Once the matter was posed in this manner, Justin had no other option than to declare that the logos was the intermediary between God and the world and was therefore a being whose status was somewhere between the immutable God and this transitory world. The manner in which Justin stated this was by speaking of the logos as "another God."[8] Although such language would obviously be abandoned soon, the basic statement and understanding of the situation became increasingly common, to the point that by the time of the Council of Nicea it seems to have been taken for granted by a vast number of bishops and theologians that God was by nature immutable, in contrast to the mutable Word.

It was out of this context that Arianism arose. The traditional view, that Arianism was an attempt to reaffirm Jewish monotheism and that it arose out of Judaizing tendencies, is now rejected by most scholars. I would add that such a notion, which appeared while the controversy was still raging, was the result of antisemitic bias, which sought to pin the origin of this and other heresies on Jews and Judaizers. The fact of the matter is that both Arius and his opponents were much influenced by Greek philosophy. Arius's basic scheme was one in which God the Father was immutable, and the Word was the mutable intermediary between that God and the obviously mutable world. Although he did affirm the monotheism that was essential to the Judeo-Christian tradition—and that his opponents also affirmed—the issue was not one of numbers, of whether God is one or not, but rather one having to do with the status of the Word.[9]

What most disturbed Arius was not the possibility that this other one—namely, the Word of God—might also be called God, but rather that such a declaration would make God mutable, for it was clear, especially through the incarnation, that the Word of God was mutable. The Arian assertion that "there was when [the Word] was not" was designed to show that the reason why the Word could relate directly with this mutable world, and even—in the incarnation—become part of it, was precisely that the Logos—unlike the eternal Father—was mutable and created.

When the Council of Nicea was convened to deal with the controversy, it was clear that the Council was an imperial affair. It was the emperor who called it and presided over it. The bishops traveled from their sees to Nicea at imperial expense. When the Council came together, it was evident that neither Constantine nor most of the bishops present had a

105

very clear idea of what the discussion was all about. What was clear to Constantine, and what he made crystal clear to the bishops, was that the Council must not adjourn without resolving the issue and restoring peace to the church. Constantine did not seem to care who was right, as long as all agreed. But as the debate evolved and the Arian position became known, most bishops agreed that it was necessary to affirm the full divinity of the Son or Word of God. Eventually, a creed was formulated which asserted that the Son was "God from God, light from light, true God from true God," and "of one substance with the Father" (*homoousios tō patri*). It is also significant that although the Caesarean creed that was probably used as a model for the Creed of Nicea spoke of the "Word" or "logos" of God, the Council preferred to speak of the "Son." Thus while not rejecting the doctrine of the logos, which by then had had a long history in Christian theology, the bishops showed their preference for the more personal term "Son."

Scholars who interpret the early history of Christian thought in terms of the progressive deification of Jesus see in the Council of Nicea his final apotheosis. And it is true that this was an unusually clear statement of the divinity of Jesus—a divinity that was declared to be equal with the Father's. But in another sense this seeming "promotion" of the Son could be seen as a "demotion" of the entire Godhead. Even though perhaps unwittingly, the Council refused to accept uncritically the supposed immutability and impassibility of God, and the doctrine that it promulgated would forever remind the church of the difference between the active, living God of Scripture and the fixed "first cause" or "Supreme Being" of the philosophers and of much of Christian theology. What the bishops said at Nicea was that this One who "for us and for our salvation came down and became incarnate, becoming man, suffered and rose again on the third day," this One is "God from God, light from light, true God from true God, . . . of one substance with the Father." How then can the divine substance be conceived of in fixed, static terms? For generations, Christians would be discomfited by this statement, which they took to be authoritative and which yet spoke of the Godhead in terms hardly compatible with the notion of God that theology itself had come to regard as normative.

The inconsistency of the Nicene position has often been pointed out and was one of the main arguments of the Arian party against the decisions of the Council. Indeed, the bishops gathered at Nicea were trapped within the ontologist and static notion of God that had already become dominant, but they refused to carry that notion of God to its ultimate consequences. Rather, they introduced an insurmountable obstacle in the way of any who would attempt to draw such consequences: The Son of God, the One whom we have seen, touched, and handled in Jesus Christ, is "of one substance with the Father." Thus the gospel of the minority God was preserved even as enormous forces were reshaping the very notion of God in order to adjust it to the new status enjoyed by Christians.

On this point, Arianism was more consistent than the Nicene position. According to the Arians, God was immutable and therefore did not relate directly to the world. As an intermediary between the two, there was the Logos of God, a mutable yet preexistent creature who had become incarnate in Jesus. This seemingly consistent position, however, did involve greater difficulties than it solved, as was amply shown by its opponents.

In order to show the reasons why the Nicene party opposed Arianism and the view of the Godhead involved in it, it may be helpful to take a brief look at the theology of that party's main leader, Athanasius. Those who claim that Arius was a staunch defender of monotheism over against the veiled polytheism of the Nicene party are hard pressed to show how their thesis is compatible with the constant emphasis Athanasius placed on monotheism. Indeed, one of the recurrent themes in the writings of Athanasius was the existence of a single God. The other main theme was that salvation must come from God. It was on the basis of these two presuppositions, which he saw as standing at the heart of the Christian faith, that Athanasius felt compelled to reject the Arian position. If the Arian logos is a creature, we are indebted to a creature, and not to God, for our salvation. If, on the other hand, the Arian logos is divine, and yet not of the same substance as the Father, we end up with two gods. Furthermore, Athanasius rejected the entire Arian construct, for once one says that the function of the Logos or Word of God is to serve as an intermediary between the immutable God and the mutable world, one is still left with the problem of needing another intermediary between the immutable God and the mutable logos, and so on, ad infinitum. Over against the Arian position, therefore, Athanasius insisted on the direct communication of God with creation, and particularly with human creatures. Although God is transcendent, this is not to be understood in such a way that God cannot relate to the world and to human beings. Thus while Athanasius never flatly denied the immutability of God, it is clear that he could not accept the Arian position precisely because, taking that immutability as its point of departure, it made it impossible for God to communicate directly with humankind. The difference between the Father and the Son could not be described as that which exists between the immutable and the mutable.

In any case, the decision made at Nicea had political consequences that went far beyond the obvious. The obvious was that the Council had been gathered at Constantine's command and that it would have preferred not to have decided on the issue at all. The not so obvious was that its decision and the doctrine that it promulgated had—like every doctrine—political overtones. What was in fact affirmed by the Council was that the "very God of very God" had become incarnate in a Jewish carpenter who was then condemned to death by the Roman Empire and the powerful of his time. This was the God whom the emperor had espoused. And all the while Constantine, and several Christian leaders around him, were trying to make it appear that the emperor was godlike and that God was emperorlike. In the Roman imperial tradition, Constantine was assured of a place in the pantheon of the gods—and indeed, in spite of his conversion, after his death he was declared to be a god. It was precisely the divinity of the emperor that had been one of the bulwarks of imperial power, as well as one of the main reasons why Christians had been persecuted. Constantine was not about to exchange such a privileged position for that of the follower of an outlawed and executed carpenter. The exaltation of God was important to him and to his successors, for it was also the exaltation of the emperors who had become God's champions and representatives. If a carpenter condemned to death as an outlaw, someone who had nowhere to lay his head, was declared to be "very God of very God," such a declaration would put in doubt the very view of God and of hierarchy on which imperial power rested.

Therefore, it is not surprising to see that very soon after the Council adjourned, Constantine had second thoughts about its decisions. At the time of the Council, he had ordered Arius banished; a few years later he was ordering the bishop of Constantinople to readmit Arius to communion. From that point on, Constantine lent increasing support to the Arian party in its efforts to have the decisions of Nicea set aside. Finally, he was baptized on his deathbed by Eusebius of Nicomedia, the foremost leader of the Arian party, who by then had also become one of the emperor's most trusted advisers in religious matters.

It is not necessary to recount here the political vicissitudes of the controversy. Let it suffice to point out that, although both sides made use of political pressure in their efforts to gain the upper hand, in general it was the Arians who received more open support from the emperors who favored them. During the time of Constantius, it became evident that most church leaders were opposed to Arianism, and yet the emperor saw fit to favor that doctrine to the point of forcing several bishops to sign Arian—or quasi-Arian—declarations of faith. In this he was showing keen political intuition, for the Arian impassible God, clearly different from the passible and second-rate Son or Word of God, was more supportive of imperial authority than the living God of Scripture, even in the mitigated Nicene form.

The Patripassian Alternative

It is significant, however, that the doctrine that really gained adherents among the masses was not Arianism but Patripassianism. This was the view of those who held that there was no distinction between the Father and the Son. Although Patripassianism took different forms, in general it held that the Father, Son, and Holy Spirit were three "modes" or "faces" of the same God. This God had appeared as Father in the Old Testament, as Son in Jesus Christ, and now as Spirit in the life of the church. Its opponents called this doctrine Patripassianism, because it implied that the Father had suffered the passion of Christ. They often argued against it on the basis that it made God passible, thus inadvertently playing into the hand of the Arians. What these opponents of Patripassianism did not seem to realize was that the reason this doctrine was so attractive to so many in the church was that it showed clearly that God was one of their number. God was not like the emperor and his nobles, who had an easy life in their lofty positions. God had toiled and suffered even as they must toil and suffer every day. On this point, it would seem that the Patripassians had an insight into the nature of the biblical God that the more powerful leaders of the church had begun to lose.

On the other hand, this does not mean that the eventual rejection of Patripassianism by the church at large was a mistake. In clearly asserting the suffering of God, Patripassianism was right. But in denying the distinction between Father and Son it lost the dialectic of power and powerlessness, of suffering and hope, which is central to the Christian doctrine of redemption. Indeed, what makes the suffering of Christ a sign of hope is that, even in the midst of his suffering, next to him stands a Father who is to raise him from the dead. What makes his powerlessness so powerful is precisely that while God is being crucified in the Son, the same God is also upholding the entire universe—and even those who crucify Jesus—in the Father.

The other point at which Patripassianism was questionable was in that it made the incarnation only a passing stage. God was made human but did not remain so. Over against this, the church held that the incarnation was not a passing moment in the life of God. God did not take on humanity for thirty-three years in order simply to discard it as a used garment. The incarnation did not end with the crucifixion and resurrection. On the contrary, what the doctrine of ascension meant was that God is still human, that even now one of us, a carpenter, an outlaw, a convicted and executed criminal, sits "at the right hand" of the Father. Because of the incarnation, when we now look at God we are not looking at an entirely alien being but at one of us. The exile whose body was wrecked in the mines of ancient Pontus as well as the one whose body is now wrecked in the lettuce fields of California can look to the Godhead and say, "One of us reigns in glory, and as he reigns, we too are called to reign." Here one is reminded of the passage in Hebrews 2, where the author comments that although we do not yet rule as we are intended to, "we see Jesus, who for a little while was made lower than the angels, crowned with glory and honor because of the suffering of death, so that by the grace of God he might taste death for every one" (Heb. 2:9). The continuing life of the Crucified, now in power and glory, is the promise and the calling of all those who are now suffering oppression like he suffered.

Eventually the Nicene party won the struggle against both Arianism and Patripassianism. The triumph over Arianism ensured that even amid the majority church of the Middle Ages and of modern times, the voice would be heard of the minority God who was made flesh in a humble carpenter belonging to an oppressed nation. The victory over Patripassianism assured Christians of all ages that suffering, oppression, and despair do not have the last word, for behind the suffering Son and suffering humankind stands the One who vindicates the Son and all those who, like him, suffer oppression and injustice; that at the right hand of the throne of glory stands the Lamb of God, in representation of all those who are like lambs taken to the slaughter. But the profound insight of this Nicene faith was often overshadowed by the fact that Christians had now become a powerful body and would soon be literally a majority. Since the church—or at least its leaders—now had power, it tended to identify its God with the God of the powerful—that is, with the Impassible One who by virtue of seemingly neutral inactivity sacralizes the status quo. To this day, the church may be separated from the state, but it certainly is not always separated from the structures of privilege and injustice that the state often embodies.

Hispanic Americans are becoming increasingly aware of this situation. This in turn is leading some to abandon the Christian faith altogether, as either oppressive or at best inoperative in a situation of oppression. And there is no doubt that faith in a "prime unmoved mover" or a "Supreme Being" may well be a means of sacralizing oppression. But faith in the living God of the Bible, in the Crucified One who is "of one substance with the Father," has enormous liberating and subversive power. It is faith in a God who joins the dispossessed in their struggle and marches with them to victory, liberation, and new life. It is faith in the God who is a minority and who therefore speaks Spanish. When Hispanics wish to ask another to speak clearly or to speak Spanish, we often say, "Habla en cristiano" (speak in Christian). This is obviously a relic of the seven centuries during which Spanish Christian and Moslem Moor confronted each other in the Iberian Peninsula. It is also a reminder of an age when those who spoke Spanish were the most powerful people on the face of the earth, and they could assume—as some Anglo-Americans seem to assume now—that God preferred their language. But in the present situation in these United States, this phrase may be taken as a sign that God does indeed speak Spanish, not in the sense of speaking this language in preference to others but in the biblical sense that the oppressed who speak Spanish—like those who speak black English—are given a special hearing. In Peru, God probably speaks Quechua rather than Spanish. In this country the God whose supreme revelation takes place in a carpenter from Galilee is seen primarily not in the stained-glass windows of the rich suburban church but in the Chicano lettuce or grape picker who is denied the right to unionize; in the suffering of the Puerto Rican in a Chicago tenement house; in the pain of those who are constantly told, in a thousand different ways, that their culture and language are inferior, and that they must conform to the language and culture of the majority—which is no more than a veiled way of saying that they must be reconciled with the fact that they will always be inferior. God hears and understands. This we know because the One who is "God from God, light from light, very God from very God" was crucified, died, and was buried, and the third day rose from the dead and ascended unto heaven, where he sits in power, and from whence he shall come again to judge the powerful and the powerless.

An "Economic" Doctrine of the Trinity

In classical theological jargon, the distinction is often made between an "economic" and an "immanent" (or "essential") doctrine of the Trinity. These terms, on whose meaning not all agree, are usually employed to distinguish between one view that holds that the Trinity is "essential" to God and another which holds that it refers only to God's revelation and relations with creation. Thus stated, the debate seems pointless, for we have no way of knowing how God is in Godself, and therefore to speak of an "essential" Trinity, apart from God's revelation and relations with the world, is nonsense.

Perhaps, however, there is another way in which we should speak of an "economic" doctrine of the Trinity. In this other approach, what we should ask is, What are the socioeconomic consequences of the doctrine of the Trinity? If there are any such consequences, it is clear that the doctrine of the Trinity, far from being the idle speculation of theologians with nothing better to do, is rather a view of God that has drastic consequences for the manner in which we are to order our society and economic relations within it.

When I first studied the history of the Trinitarian debates, I had great difficulty understanding their significance. My professors, mostly schooled in the tradition of Harnack, had little sympathy for seemingly endless discussions as to whether or not the Son was consubstantial with the Father. The controversies themselves, and particularly the comment of Gregory Nazianzen that one couldn't even have one's shoes repaired without getting into a discussion as to the begetting of the Son, seemed to my professors and to me no more than another instance of the strange penchant of the human psyche for idle fanaticism. However, as years have gone by, I have begun to question that superior attitude of the nineteenth and twentieth centuries. Perhaps the reason why the debate seemed so frivolous to us was that we did not understand some of the dimensions involved. My first approach, true to the schooling I had received, was to seek to understand the philosophical and theological issues more profoundly. This gave me greater appreciation for the theological issues involved, and in particular for the arguments of Athanasius relating soteriology with the doctrine of the Trinity. But still there seemed to be an element that eluded me.

Then, on a completely different project, I began studying the social and economic teachings of the great theologians of the fourth century who had also been the champions of Trinitarian theology. And I found some rather surprising views:

Ambrose, comparing Christian doctrine with that of the philosophers:

> They [the philosophers] considered it consonant with justice that one should treat common, that is, public property as public, and private as private. But this is not in accord with nature, for nature has poured forth all things for all people for common use. God has ordered all things to be produced, so that there should be food in common to all, and that the earth should be a common possession for all. Nature, therefore, has produced a common right for all, but greed has made it a right for a few.[10]

Jerome:

I agree with the popular saying, that one is rich either through one's own injustice or by inheriting from an unjust person.[11]

In the East, Basil the Great:

The beasts become fertile when they are young, but quickly cease to be so. But capital produces interest from the very beginning, and this in turn multiplies into infinity. All that grows ceases to do so when it reaches its normal size. But the money of the greedy never stops growing.[12]

Finally, Gregory Nazianzen:

After sin came into the world, greed destroyed the original nobility of nature, and turned law into the handmaiden of the powerful. But you, do look to the original equality, not to the latter distinction; not to the law of the powerful, but to the law of the Creator.[13]

The quotations could go on endlessly. But the basic point should be clear by now: Could there be a connection between these people's social and economic doctrine, radical as it was, and their staunch defense of the doctrine of the Trinity?

The answer is obvious. The commonality that exists within the Trinity is the pattern and goal of creation and is therefore the example that those who believe in the Trinity are called to follow. Tanzanian Roman Catholic bishop Christopher Mwoleka put it very succinctly in his defense of *Ujamaa*, the Tanzanian form of socialism. He argued that Christians have made the basic mistake of approaching the Trinity as a puzzle to be solved rather than as an example to be imitated.

Although Bishop Mwoleka does not say so, it is clear that the approach to the Trinity that he criticizes has been fostered by theologians and by the clergy as a means to retain power, and that part of the result has been that the faith has been taken away from the common folk—with the by-product that popular religiosity has turned to those items and practices that more "sophisticated" Christians term "superstition."[14] The doctrine of the Trinity, when approached in this manner, certainly has an oppressive quality, and it has been used throughout the centuries to overwhelm folk by surrounding the Trinity with a sense of mystery that only the clergy can understand, and also, even among the clergy, to condemn as heretics those whom one wished to bring down for other reasons.[15]

Over against such a view and use of the doctrine of the Trinity, Mwoleka rightly declared that God does not give us riddles for speculation but examples for imitation:

I am dedicated to the ideal of Ujamaa because it invites everyone, in a down to earth practical way, to imitate the life of the Trinity which is a life of sharing.

The three Divine Persons share everything in such a way that there are not three gods but only one God. And Christ's wish is: "That they (his followers) may be one as we are one. With me in them and you in me, may they be completely one. . . ."

On believing in this mystery, the first thing we should have done was to imitate God, then we would ask no more questions, for we would understand. God does not reveal Himself to us for the sake of speculation. He is not giving us a riddle to solve. He is offering us life. He is telling us: "This is what it means to live, now begin to live as I do." What is the one and only reason why God revealed this mystery to us if it is not to stress that life is not life at all unless it is shared?[16]

If this is so, the connection between the radical socioeconomic views quoted above and the doctrine of the Trinity seems obvious, as does also the opposition to Trinitarian doctrine of many among the powerful in the fourth century. If the Trinity is the doctrine of a God whose very life is a life of sharing, its clear consequence is that those who claim belief in such a God must live a similar life. And it is true that from a very early date the doctrine of the Trinity was developed in terms of sharing. Tertullian, the first to use the Latin term *Trinitas*, as well as the formula that would eventually become classic, "one substance and three persons," argued that what made these three persons one was their sharing of a common substance, and he even offered examples taken from the sharing of a common possession by more than one.[17] He has been criticized for using terminology and examples drawn from legal usage, rather than metaphysical terminology and examples. But perhaps this is reason for commendation rather than criticism.

Tertullian, by the way, was the theologian who introduced the Greek word *oikonomia* into Latin theological discourse, arguing that "even though he is the one only God, one must believe in him with his own *oikonomia*."[18] The term *oikonomia*, which later theologians have employed to refer to a "nonessential" Trinity, here means "administration, inner management, arrangement." Thus what Tertullian is saying is that the One God exists according to an inner order, and that this order is best understood in terms of the sharing of a *substantia*—which in the legal terminology of that time could mean "property"—by three persons. Thus what he meant by *oikonomia* may not be all that distant from what I mean here by an "economic" doctrine of the Trinity. And it is significant to note that he also gave great importance to sharing among Christians, who according to him are "of one mind and soul, and do not hesitate to share earthly possessions among [themselves], for all things, except wives, are held in common among [them]."[19]

The doctrine of the Trinity, once cleared of the stale metaphysical language in which it has been couched, affirms belief in a God whose essence is sharing. "God is love," says the First Epistle of John. And the doctrine of the Trinity also says, "God is love." This love of God, however, is not only something we receive, or something we must praise. It is also something we must imitate, for if God is love, life without love is life without God; and if this is a sharing love, such as we see in the Trinity, then life without sharing is life without God; and if this sharing is such that in God the three persons are equal in power, then life without such power sharing is life without God.

This must be carried beyond the purely individual, and therefore those of us who believe in the God who is love, in the Triune God, must also affirm that a society—or a church—in which such love is not manifest is a society—or a church—without God.

As Hispanics today look at the doctrine of the Trinity, we would do well to set aside interpretations that see it in purely speculative or metaphysical terms and seek to discover, to imitate, and to apply to our societal and ecclesiastical life the love of the Triune God. And, as in so many other matters, we should seek to be a "bridge people," helping our white sisters and brothers in the North Atlantic understand the significance of this insight for the life and faith of the entire church catholic.

CHAPTER 8

Creator of Heaven and Earth

The Apostles' Creed, which affirms belief in God the Parent all-ruling—*pantokrator*—also affirms that this God is the Creator of heaven and earth. Since we are part of creation and it is within creation that our entire existence takes place, it is important that we explore the significance of that creedal statement.

The Goodness of Creation

The first obvious consequence of the doctrine of creation is that the creature has a positive value. The early church insisted that God is "all-ruling" and "maker of heaven and earth" precisely because there were those who denied this. Heaven and earth are not the result of an error or sin. They are the result of the will of God. As Genesis repeatedly states, when God made each thing, "God saw that it was good."

Thus the doctrine of creation is first of all an affirmation of the positive value of the world, and a rejection of any doctrine or theory that diminishes or denies that value. Christians, like others, have often been tempted to flee to an otherworldly religion. But the doctrine of creation affirms that *this* is the world God made and declared to be good. One can certainly say—one must certainly say—that it is tainted by sin. But there is no other world, no other cosmos, than this heaven and earth that God has made. To flee from it as if there were some other reality is not only a mistake; it is also an impossibility.

The created cosmos, in which we must exist and of which we are part, includes "heaven and earth." Too often this is interpreted to mean that beyond this passing "earth," tainted by sin and temporality, there is an eternal "heaven," unblemished and unfading. It is on this basis that

Christian escapism usually functions, inviting people to flee from the cares of this earth and look to the heavenly rewards. But the fact of the matter is that according to Scripture both heaven and earth are temporal creations of God, both will equally pass, and both are tainted by sin. The notion that earth below is a passing "vale of tears" and that heaven above is an abiding place of pure bliss is not warranted by Scripture. In Luke 10:18, Jesus tells his disciples that, at the time of their preaching and presumably as the result of it, he saw Satan fall from heaven. In Revelation 12, the "great red dragon" is in heaven, and the reason for the present woes on earth is precisely that the devil has been expelled from heaven, which until now has been his abode. Finally, at the end of the same book, we are promised not only a new earth, but also a new heaven.

That God is creator of "heaven and earth" means also that we are part of creation. In the next chapter we shall explore further the meaning of our humanity. But here it may be useful to remind ourselves that we do not stand outside of creation. We cannot escape the created order precisely because we too are creatures. It is here, in this created cosmos, both on earth and in heaven, that we are to live and to serve God.

Creation Is Not God

The second consequence of the doctrine of creation is that God and creation are two distinct realities. The one does not flow naturally from the other, nor does the other lead simply and directly to the one. As the theologians of the fourth century put it, creation is not of the "essence" but of the "will" of God. This became important at the time as a manner of affirming that the Word of God, the Second Person of the Trinity, is divine. The cosmos, they said, is "made" or "created" and is the result of the "will" of God. The Word, on the other hand, is "begotten, not made" and "of the essence of the Father"—both phrases from the Nicene Creed. Creation does not flow from God's substance, like the series of emanations that the Neoplatonists posited.

If creation were a series of emanations from the divine substance, it would be hierarchically ordered, with some creatures by their very nature standing closer to God than others. But creation is not an emanation of the divine substance. It is rather the result of the sovereign divine will. Creatures are not ordered in such a way that by their very nature they stand at various distances from God. Ontologically, every created being is infinitely distant from the being of God.

The view that there is a hierarchy of being and that as one climbs along that hierarchy one approaches God was very prevalent during the Middle Ages. Partly through the influence of Pseudo-Dionysius, who was thought to have been a direct disciple of the Apostle Paul, all reality was seen as a series of ordered hierarchies, and the goal of the Christian life was precisely to ascend along those hierarchies. Many of the great classics of Christian mysticism, such as Bonaventure's *Itinerarium mentis in Deum*, are built on this premise. Such a view of the cosmos and its order, however, stands closer to the Neoplatonic theory of emanation than to the Christian doctrine of creation.

The significance of this is that God is not reached, so to speak, by climbing to the highest point of creation. The baals of the Older Testament were to be found on the hilltops. The God of Israel speaks on Mount Sinai, but also in the lowlands of Egypt and Babylon. And what is true in geographical terms is also true in terms of ontological and social standing.

When it comes to social standing, the God of Israel speaks to King David and King Solomon on their thrones, but also to Amos among the shepherds of Tekoa. God remains sovereign over creation, and one does not necessarily approach the Creator the more one advances along a supposed hierarchy of creatures, be that a geographical, ontological, ecclesiastical, or sociopolitical hierarchy.

Hispanics are well aware of this. In every human society there is a tendency to think that the "high and mighty" are closer to God. The church does not often escape from the same tendency. In the denomination to which I belong, this has led to the strange practice of naming churches after large donors—a practice that Christians in centuries past would have found shocking. (For this reason, very few United Methodist churches will ever be named after Hispanics or other minorities.) In every denomination, power and prestige in society at large translates into power and prestige in the church. It is as if a higher standing in the social hierarchy were an indication of a closer connection to God. Thus while we do not lift up our eyes to the holy places where the baals are worshiped, we are often invited, by the church itself, to lift up our eyes to the stories of success where today's baals are worshiped.

Creation, however, is not a hierarchical order that leads to the divine as a ladder leads to the attic. In the act of creation, God remains sovereign. The sovereign God who chooses to speak not in the mighty wind but in a whisper, not directly to King Jeroboam but to Amos among the shepherds of Tekoa, has also chosen to speak in a Galilean carpenter who makes the astonishing claim, "Who has seen me has seen the Father"—and who also says and repeats the astonishingly antihierarchi-

119

cal words, "The last shall be first" and "Among you the one who serves is the greatest."

To say that creation is good is to say that we cannot escape it, and should not even try to escape it. To say that it is not God is to say that its present order is not final.

Heaven and Earth

"Heaven and earth," says the Creed. This may be interpreted in a number of ways. It could mean simply the physical planet (earth) and everything that surrounds it (heaven). For our purposes, however, there is another dimension of this phrase that bears underlining. "Heaven *and* earth" means that this physical earth that we see—the planet Earth, the solar system, the galaxies, and all that space encompasses—is not the totality of creation. There is also "heaven," not in the sense of "a place up there" but rather in the sense of those dimensions of creation that our mind cannot encompass.[1]

Here, we must avoid two positions that seem to be diametrically opposed to each other but that in truth often lead to the same practical consequences. The first is the escapist, spiritualizing position that has already been mentioned. From this perspective, there are two places, heaven and earth. Earth is the physical place where we live in bodies, and where events occur that have significance only inasmuch as they open or close the way to heaven. Heaven is another place where spirits abide, and where our souls will live eternally if we gain admission while we live on earth. We have already shown that such a view of heaven has little biblical warrant.

A second view is that, after all, there is nothing but the physical, empirical, measurable world, and that what the Creed refers to is the earth and the sky—or, in more modern terms, our planet and the space around it. It is true that when Scripture speaks of "heaven," it often means little more than the sky. But normally "heaven" is much more than that. Heaven is a hidden order of reality that reminds us that the empirical, predictable, measurable earth is not the totality of creation. God the *pantocrator* rules not only over earth but also over heaven. The struggle against sin and its power takes place not only on earth but also in heaven.

What this means is that the "earth" that we can see, measure, understand, and rule is only part of God's creation. Next to the earth, above, under, and around it, stands this other dimension of creation, "heaven."

This is of crucial importance for Hispanic piety and theology. We hear much these days about the "modern" notion of a "closed universe." We are told that since the mechanistic view of the universe seems to work, and since in any case we can only think in terms of cause and effect, it is senseless to speak in terms of divine intervention in history. The universe is closed to divine intervention and works only on the basis of unalterable laws that cannot be changed or suspended. Thus part of "modernity" is to believe in such a closed universe. As Rudolf Bultmann has put it, "It is impossible to use electric light and the wireless and to avail ourselves of modern medical and surgical discoveries, and at the same time to believe in the New Testament world of spirits and miracles."[2]

The fact, however, is that it is not only possible but even common. All over the world, and certainly in the Hispanic believing community, people use not only electric light and the wireless but computers and laser printers to tell about the wondrous things that God has done in their lives.

Is this simply a matter of willful denial of what should be self-evident to any thinking person, as Bultmann would have us believe? Or is there more to it? One could argue that the view that the universe is closed and its workings are like those of a machine is part of the ideology by which those who control the present order destroy or curtail the hope of those whose only hope lies in change. "Modern reason" precludes our thinking in terms of divine intervention. But by whose standards of "modernity" and whose definition of "reason"?[3]

The fact is that ever since Kant, we have been aware of the degree to which our reason imposes its limits on the world—how we say, for instance, that causality is a "law of nature" because it is a law of our own reason. With the work of Freud, Marx, and their successors, it has also become clear that "reason" does not function in a vacuum but is conditioned by historical, psychological, socioeconomic, and other factors. We have also learned that "reason" can hide those factors from itself and thus convince itself that its conclusions are the result of "pure reason." Thus when "reason" seems to require that we believe in a "closed universe," one that is impervious to anything but mechanistic laws, one begins to wonder whether this is not a definition of "reason" that is designed as a defense of the status quo, and as a means to discourage those whose strength comes from the hope of divine intervention.

To such a closed view of the universe, we answer that God is the creator of heaven and earth, and that the earth that the mind can encompass and manipulate to its own ends is but a part of the whole—a part whose very nature is misunderstood when it is taken for the whole.

In summary, to say that God is the creator of earth *and heaven* is to say that earth does not exhaust the reality of creation. Earth, as that which we can understand and manage, is only part of that reality. According to the workings of earth, the powerful will remain powerful since they control the mechanisms of nature and of history. But there are also the workings of *heaven,* the mysterious and uncontrollable dimension of creation.

To say, on the other hand, that God is the creator of heaven *and earth* is to say that the rational, predictable workings of earth are also part of God's creation, and that one cannot serve God without seeking to employ those workings for God's ends.

Both of these are an important part of a genuine Hispanic spirituality. All one has to do is attend a Hispanic worship service or prayer meeting to come to the conclusion that the Hispanic universe is not closed, that it is not limited to "earth" but has a very strong element of trust in the workings of "heaven." If anything, some of us are sometimes tempted to give up on "earth" and its workings, which so often are employed against us. But when so tempted, we are corrected by our faith in "God the Parent all-ruling, maker of heaven and earth."

Creation and Evolution

There is much debate these days about the theory of evolution and its relation to the doctrine of creation. This is not the place to join that debate, but there are two points that require clarification, especially inasmuch as they touch on Hispanic experience and theology.

The first of these is that the debate tends to reduce the doctrine of creation to what should properly be named "the beginning of creation."[4] Creation, properly understood, is not something that took place sometime in the past—be it six thousand or six billion years ago—and that now is a matter of antiquarian curiosity or fanatical orthodoxy. Creation has to do both with the beginning and with the continued existence of heaven and earth. One should not suppose that God was Creator only in the beginning and has now relinquished that role in favor of Sustainer. Creation subsists, even now, because God has called it and continues calling it out of nothingness into being. Without the sustaining and creating Word of God, heaven and earth would not subsist for an instant. The doctrine of creation, therefore, is not merely a statement about origins; it is also and foremost a statement about present reality and present responsibility.

The second point that needs clarification is the meaning of "evolution," and the reason why much of what is understood by that term is indeed antibiblical. The problem with evolution is not that it claims that it took God so many billions of years to bring the world to its present state—in fact, God is still not finished with the world, and "it does not yet appear what we are to be." The problem with the theory of evolution, at least in its most popular versions, is that it asserts that the ultimate rule of creation is the survival of the fittest. This is indeed antibiblical. The ultimate rule of creation is the victory of love. Nowhere is this more clearly shown than in the resurrection of Jesus Christ, destroyed as unfit by the fittest empire of his time and yet risen again from the dead.

To claim that the ultimate rule of the universe is the survival of the fittest is to assert that the process whereby the powerful and the successful oppress and destroy the powerless is part of the evolutionary process by which a better world is created. It is for this reason, and not because it speaks of millions of years instead of seven days, that we as Hispanics must denounce the simplistic evolutionary schemes that so often pass for science. We denounce and reject them because they have gone beyond the point of biological theory and have become the justification of social policy.

123

CHAPTER 9

On Being Human

Just like every other Christian doctrine, the notion of what it means to be human—in traditional terms, the doctrine of "man"—has been used in oppressive ways. Thus as we seek to do theology from a Hispanic perspective, we must look again at this doctrine, both in its historical development and in the hidden agendas which that development has served.

Body and Soul

Most of us, when asked about Christian anthropology, will probably think first of all about the notion that a human being is a composite of body and soul. Others will remember that there is also the option of speaking of "body, soul, and spirit." Thus a fundamental debate would seem to be whether we are to conceive of human nature as consisting of two parts or of three—in traditional terms, whether we hold to a "dichotomist" or a "trichotomist" anthropology. A trichotomist anthropology was rejected by the Fourth Council of Constantinople (869–870) in its eleventh canon.[1] For that reason, as well as for what seems to be overwhelming biblical support, most theologians since that time have opted for a dichotomist view. The fact of the matter is that both views can claim the support of the New Testament, which usually speaks in terms of body and soul (Matt. 10:28), but where there is also a text that speaks of body, soul, and spirit (I Thess. 5:23). This should suffice to alert us to the possibility that no matter what may have been the views of various biblical authors on this matter, this certainly is not the basic issue of biblical anthropology, and that perhaps in asking the question in this manner we are asking the wrong question.

Here again, as in the case of the doctrine of God, what has been done is to pose in ontological terms what the Bible poses in a different manner. The Bible is not interested in the body and the soul, or in the body, the soul, and the spirit, as constitutive parts of the human creature. The Bible is not interested in how many parts there are to us, or in how they relate to each other, but rather in the divine purposes for our lives, and how we can be obedient to such purposes. As José Ortega y Gasset would say, "A human being is not a thing, but a drama."[2]

In order to understand why the question of the soul as a substance came to be so important for Christian theology, it is necessary to return once again to the formative centuries of Christian theology. Christians were ridiculed for their ignorance, and particularly for the obstinacy they showed in being willing to face death rather than abandon their faith. Obviously, one of the reasons why Christians had such fortitude was that they were convinced that they would live again (another reason, not directly pertinent to our present discussion, was that they were also convinced that in their martyrdom Christ suffered with them and thus alleviated their pain). This insistence on life after death made them subject to further ridicule, for it seemed to many nothing but a chimera. Why, asked their critics, give up this life, which is certain, for a dubious life to come?

In response to such questioning, Christians had recourse to the Greek philosophical tradition, whose most respected exponents had spoken of life after death. Socrates' insistence that neither those who accused him nor the poison they forced him to take could destroy his soul, and the calmness with which he approached death, were then used by Christians as proof that the wisest among the philosophers agreed with them.

But, once again, such apologetic bridges can bear traffic in both directions, and what began as an argument to convince unbelievers became part of accepted Christian doctrine. Therefore, although Christians still spoke of the resurrection of the body, which had been part of their faith from the beginning, they also began to think of the future life in terms of the immortality of the soul.[3] The truth of the matter is that the Bible nowhere says that the soul is immortal. On the contrary, Jesus speaks of one who can "kill the soul" (Matt. 10:28). In most cases, the Bible uses the term "soul" as another way of speaking of one's entire being, without any attempt to distinguish it from the body or to enter into discussions as to how many parts constitute a human being. Thus the Psalmist, for instance, can speak of both "soul" and "bones" as one's very being:

126

Then my soul shall rejoice in the Lord,
    exulting in his deliverance.
All my bones shall say,
    "O Lord, who is like thee,
thou who deliverest the weak
    from him who is too strong for him,
    the weak and the needy from him who despoils him?"(Ps. 35:9–10)

This is clear in the New Testament, where sometimes we are told that Jesus gave "himself" for us (Gal. 1:4; Eph. 5:2, 25), while at other times we are told that he gave his "soul" (John 10:11; Matt. 20:28; the Revised Standard Version here translates "soul" as "life"), and in still other texts it is said that he gave his "body" (Rom. 7:4; Heb. 10:10, and the various passages of institution of the Lord's Supper). What this clearly indicates is that the soul and the body are not two different parts of a person but rather the same person as seen from different perspectives. A human being is not a soul that has taken up a body, nor a body to which has been added a soul, but a single being who is at the same time both body and soul. Karl Barth has stated this very well:

> We best keep ourselves from prejudice, abstraction and one-sidedness if we proceed from the concrete reality in which man neither lacks the inner differentiation of soul and body, nor is mere soul or mere body, nor merely a combination and association of the two, but wholly and simultaneously both body and soul, always and in every relation soulful, and always and in every relation bodily. We cannot cease to see both and therefore these two; for the unity of soul and body does not consist in their identity, or in the interchangeability of soul and bodily [sic]. But again we cannot cease to see both, and therefore the two together; for the unity of soul and body does not consist in the union of two parts which can always be seen and described separately.[4]

The Bible does not speak of human beings as divided into two "parts" or "substances." It speaks rather of a single entity that is properly understood neither in purely materialistic terms nor in purely spiritual terms. The entire human being is body, and the same human being is soul. A disembodied soul is not a human being, just as a "dis-souled" body is no longer a human being.

In any case, what is clear is that no matter whether there are three, two, or only one constitutive part to the human creature, this is not the main concern of Scripture when speaking about that creature. Nor is it the main concern of Scripture when speaking about "salvation."

It is also clear that the notion of the soul as the true being of the human creature, temporarily dwelling in a body, has no biblical basis. The doctrine of the immortality of the soul, which so often passes for

127

Christian orthodoxy, is no more biblical than the doctrines of the preexistence and transmigration of souls. As a matter of fact, historically and logically these three tenets regarding the soul—preexistence, immortality, and transmigration—are interconnected. Therefore, it is strange that so many Christians have accepted one while rejecting the other two.

What is most significant for our present purpose, however, is that the common understanding of the human being as consisting of two (or three) parts is not a sociopolitically neutral notion. On the contrary, it has been used and is still used to justify oppression. Once one divides human nature into two parts, one physical and the other psychical, it is a simple matter to move on to the affirmation that the higher element in our life is the psychical. At least by implication, the physical is then downgraded and seen, if not as evil, at least as less significant or less human. Thus from the division of the human creature into two substances follows the hierarchization of those substances. This hierarchical understanding of the relationship between body and soul is so ingrained in our view of human nature that even Karl Barth, who is careful to reject the dichotomy that usually goes with it, insists on the subordination of the body to the soul. On this basis, he declares

> that it [the human creature] is not a chaos but a cosmos, in which there rules a Logos; that there is control on the one side, i.e., that of the soul, and service on the other, i.e., that of the body. As this takes place man is fully man in the unity and differentiation of his soul and his body.[5]

This hierarchical understanding of human nature was the basis for the medieval claim that the church had greater authority than the state. Note the manner in which the relationship between soul and body is applied to matters of church and state in the following words of Innocent III:

> As God the creator of the universe established two great lights in the heavens, the greater to preside over the day, and the smaller to preside over night, thus did he also establish two great authorities in the heaven of the universal church . . . the greater, that it might preside over souls as if they were days, and the lesser, that it might preside over bodies as if they were nights. These are the pontifical authority and the royal power.[6]

But quite apart from issues of church and state, this hierarchical understanding of the relation between soul and body contributes to a similarly hierarchical understanding of society. It is true that most theologians today would not hold to the simplistic dichotomy (or trichotomy) that earlier theologians quite unwittingly drew from the Greek tradition. But still, living in academic circles as most of them do

128

and having been trained in intellectual pursuits, they would hold that the greatest human achievements are those of the intellect. On this basis, men who have been doing their theology in universities and libraries have tended to look down upon the women who cook their food and the minorities who collect their garbage. Their life and work appear to them as the pure pursuit of intellectual matters, while those other folk are somehow more earthy and less developed. The academic circles in which most theology is done encourages theologians to accept the myth of the superiority of the intellectual life, and to seek to clothe it with all sorts of theological justifications.

It is on the basis of this hierarchical understanding of human achievements that some people complain about the wages of garbage collectors being close to those of university professors, forgetting that it is much more rewarding to be a professor than a garbage collector, and that therefore in all justice garbage collectors ought to be paid more than professors! Those of us who form part of the intellectual elite need to be reminded that our society could go on living for quite a while without us, but it would have a hard time surviving without those who pick lettuce, cook food, and collect garbage.

The hierarchical ordering of soul and body is then joined to the racist and sexist notion that women and people of darker skin are best suited for physical pursuits, whereas white males are best suited for the intellectual life. The obvious conclusion is that the present ordering of society—and of the "traditional" household—is grounded on human nature and ought not to be questioned. But it is clear that it can and should be questioned.[7]

A practical way to begin to question such hierarchization of soul and body would be to restore the ancient Benedictine motto, "ora et labora." If to be human is to be embodied soul and ensouled body, true human life must include a balance of the two. And if this is the biblical understanding of human nature, it may well be that theology is best done with dirt under one's fingernails. The "hermeneutical privilege of the poor" of which liberation theology speaks is grounded not only in their oppression but also in their being constantly reminded of their bodily existence by their aching bones. Therefore, it may well be that the time has come for us to begin thinking of new models of theological education and reflection that do include aching bones and dirt under the fingernails.

Body, Soul, and Ecology

The hierarchization of body and soul has also led to a devaluation of our relationship to the earth. Let us look again at the oft-quoted text of Genesis 2:7: "Then the Lord God formed man of dust from the ground, and breathed into his nostrils the breath of life; and man became a living being." Nowhere does this text indicate that there is something wrong with being made out of earth. That we are more than earth is clear from the text. But it is also clear that no matter what else we might be, we are earth. That is why God later declares, "You are dust, and to dust you shall return" (Gen. 3:19). The second part of this saying—death—is obviously the result of sin. But the first part, "You are dust," is no more than a statement of the fact that was already declared in verse 7. Being made out of dirt is not part of the curse. It is part of the original creation. It is good.

Thus from its very first chapters the Bible declares our kinship with the earth. We are not spiritual beings temporarily sojourning here. We are made of earth, and the breath of God does not destroy but rather affirms that.

There is a somewhat different creation story in the first chapter of Genesis, and there we are told that God said, when creating humankind, "Let them have dominion over the fish of the sea, and over the birds of the air, and over the cattle, and over all the earth, and over every creeping thing that creeps upon the earth" (Gen. 1:26). These words have often been interpreted as giving human beings carte blanche in their dealings with the earth. Vine Deloria, criticizing Christianity from a Native American perspective, quite correctly points out that

> it is this attitude that has been adopted wholeheartedly by Western peoples in their economic exploitation of the earth. The creation becomes a mere object when this view is carried to its logical conclusion.... Whether or not Christians wanted to carry their doctrine of man's dominance as far as it has been carried, the fact remains that the modern world is just now beginning to identify the Christian religion's failure to show adequate concern for the planet as a major factor in our present ecological crisis.[8]

Historically speaking, Deloria is correct. No other civilization has brought such destruction upon nature as has so-called Christian civilization. This has been done on the basis of the notion that we are to rule over nature. And until recent times Christian apologists would boast of the technological achievements of Western civilization as the outcome of a biblical view of our relationship to nature.[9]

On the other hand, a closer examination of the Genesis account would correct the notion that we have carte blanche in our dealings with nature. First of all, the very verse that speaks of human dominion over creation puts that dominion in a certain context: "Let us make the human in our image, after our likeness; and let them have dominion . . ." The dominion is after the likeness of God's dominion. And God's dominion, as we have already seen, is dominion in love. God does not rule the earth and humankind as a tyrant. God's very nature is being-for-others, love. If such is the case, it follows that our dominion over the earth is not that of an autocrat but rather that of self-giving governance. There is no question that humankind has enormous powers over the earth. What is surprising is that this was known as early as the time when these words were written, long before modern technology. But given the fact of that power, the biblical author sets a limit to it: It is power given to be used after the likeness of God's power. It is creative power. There is no attempt here to set a gulf between the Creator God and the human creature. Ours is a creative power that is to be used in the same manner, and in the image of, the power that has created us and still sustains us.

To this we can then add what the second narrative of creation tells us about our place in the universe. We are made of earth. That means that we do not stand over against nature but are rather part of it. We are not higher beings who can look down upon nature with utter detachment. When we look at nature, we look at ourselves, for we are part of it. One aspect of the goodness of God's creation is that we are made out of dirt—of the same dirt we undervalue and pollute. We are tied to the earth by an umbilical cord, and what good or evil we do to it we do to ourselves. Again, we are not souls visiting here from outer space but "ensouled bodies," dirt into which God breathes life.

Being for Others

In the creation narrative of Genesis 2, God begins by making heaven and earth, then Eden, and then man. All of this takes place before the creation of most of what today we would call "nature." But then God said, "It is not good that the man should be alone; I will make him a helper fit for him" (Gen. 2:18). We are so used to reading this text with reference to the creation of woman that we do not realize that between it and the passage about the rib "God formed every beast of the field and every bird of the air, and brought them to the man to see what he would call them" (Gen. 2:19). Thus for "man not to be alone" did not mean only that he should have a wife. It meant also that there should be an entire creation around him. The words "it is not good," referring to man standing by himself, contrast with the words that appear repeatedly in the other creation narrative: "And God saw that it was good" (Gen. 1:10, 12, 18, 21, 25, 31). In the first narrative, this phrase appears after the completion of each stage of creation. Now, in this second narrative, we are told that God said that it was not good "for man to be alone"—in other words, that "man" is not complete by himself. From the very act of creation, man is intended for companionship. And this companionship is not only that of the woman but also that of all creation. In and by himself, man is not "good." He is not the good creation of God.

What God then creates in order to make this lone man fully human is "a helper fit for him." Let us first of all clarify what these words mean, for they have been the object of very bad exegesis. The King James Version correctly translated this text as "a help meet" for him, meaning a fitting help. Unfortunately, our sexist society then joined the two words together, created the word "helpmeet," and into it has poured all its preconceived notions of what a wife ought to be. Such interpretation errs on two counts. First of all, the word translated as "help" has none of the connotations of a meek, docile, self-effacing "ideal" wife in the traditional sense. On the contrary, it is a word most often applied to God as the "help" of Israel. Second, what is translated as "meet" in the King James Version and as "fit" in the Revised Standard Version literally means "as in front of him." What is thus implied is something like a mirror image, a counterpart, and not necessarily a subordinate being. Actually, the difference between the woman and all the animals is precisely that they are not "fit for him." They are not bad. They are simply not equal to man. They are by nature subject to him, as is shown by the fact that he has the power of naming them.

Then comes the "rib episode," which has usually been interpreted in the sense that since the woman comes from the man, she is to be subordinate to him. But that is not the way the man in this narrative interprets the events. On the contrary, what he recognizes is that she is his counterpart, his mirror image, the one "fit for him"—or "as in front of him." And therefore he declares,

> This at last is bone of my bones
>   and flesh of my flesh;
> she shall be called Woman,
>   because she was taken out of Man. (Gen. 2:23)

What the first half of these words indicate is not lordship but recognition. Finally the man has seen his counterpart, the one "fit for him" as a mirror image. The rest of his words are not really an act of naming. He does not give her a separate name but calls her by his own name in its feminine form. He is *ish*, and she will be *ishshah*.

The man is now "good," because he has "a helper fit for him." And, as this helper is "fit" like a mirror image, she too is good, for she too has a helper fit for her. To be fully human is to be for others, and therefore God's human creature is not complete until there is another to be for.

Let me hasten to add, however, that the married couple exemplified in the story of Adam and Eve is just one of many ways in which humans fulfill one another. This story does not mean that humans are complete only in marriage. If that were so, we would have to conclude that Jesus was not fully human. Being fully human is being-for-others. This is intended to occur in our many human relationships, and not only in marriage.

It is also significant to note that, contrary to most traditional interpretations, in the Genesis text there is no hint of subordination. In the first creation narrative, all of creation is to be subordinate to the human creature, both male and female (Gen. 1:26–27). In this second narrative, the birds and the beasts are under the authority of the man, who names them, and naming is a way of having control over the named. Presumably, when the woman appears on the scene and is declared to be flesh of the man's flesh and bone of his bones, and "fit for him," she is also to share in his dominion over the creatures he has named. In any case, it is only in Genesis 3, as a result of sin, that the subjection of the woman to her husband enters the scene. It is significant to note that the man is quick to assert this power resulting from sin, for in Genesis 3:20, immediately after the curses, we are told that "the man called his wife's name Eve, because she was the mother of all living." Before, he had shared his name with her. Now he stands apart from her and names her, just as earlier he had named the birds and the beasts. From the very beginning of life after sin, the man uses his power to subject and dehumanize the woman. But in so doing he dehumanizes himself, for he no longer has a "helper fit for him," and therefore the words again apply: "It is not good for man to be alone."

The subjection of a human being to another—in this case the wife to the husband—is the result of sin, and thereof an expression of it. The creature, male and female, that in the story of Genesis 1 was to have dominion over the rest of creation was not to have dominion over its fellow human beings. In Genesis 1:26–27, it is both the male and the female that are to have dominion. But in Genesis 3, after the fall, the man claims dominion over the woman by giving her a name not his own. In this naming, they are alienated from each other. They are no longer *ish* and *ishshah*. Now she is Eve, named by Adam. Their intended for-otherness, based on their being "fit" for each other, "as in front of" each other, is now disrupted. Thus is the society of dominance born, in which we are alienated from one another precisely because we seek to lord it over one another. In such a society, it is not only the "other" that is lost. We are all lost because we have lost our for-otherness, and God has rightly said that "it is not good" for us to be for ourselves.

The Notion of Sin

Martin Luther noted that, as sinners, we know not what God is, nor what justice is, nor even what sin is. The Calvinist tradition has held a similar position in its doctrine of total depravity. Once we are this side of sin, our sinfulness so clouds both our conscience and our understanding that it is impossible for us to know what sin is. In other words, our very notion of sin is tainted by our sinfulness. This means that we must not confuse sin with crime, nor with what makes us feel guilty.

However, our society, like every society, seeks to bolster its laws and its power structure by giving them religious sanction. Therefore, there is a strong vested interest that seeks to convince us that when we break the law we commit not only a crime against the state but also a sin against God. The almighty God is turned into an ally of the mighty in our society, thus creating an almost invincible alliance. But sin is not always crime, and crime is not always sin. This has been very clear to Christians who have been a minority within any given society. In the early church, to be killed for refusing to obey the law that required that the emperor be worshiped was no sin but was rather the crown of Christian faithfulness. Moses and his followers broke the law of Egypt, from whose standpoint they were criminals. Early Christians, by having a common table at which master and slave ate together, broke the law of Rome. Martin Luther King, Jr., broke the laws of many states.

All these people should unashamedly be called criminals. They broke the law. When caught—and some of them wished to be caught— they were legally condemned. We may now say that the laws by which they were condemned were unfair. But it was the law, and they broke it. They were outlaws for God. In this they followed the same path as that convicted outlaw and executed criminal, Jesus of Nazareth. We like to say that his trial was unfair. But the truth is that, from the point of view of Roman law and order, anyone who claimed to be the Messiah of Israel was an outlaw, and as such he was tried, convicted, and executed. Those who convicted him, and those who executed him, had the legal authority to do so. He died as a criminal because he *was* a criminal, even though we may now declare that the laws that declared him to be such were unjust.

The point is that we must not confuse sin with crime. Society values law and order above everything else, mostly because those who set such values are the same people who profit from the present order and from the laws that uphold it. This is true not only of our society but of any human society this side of sin, where dominance prevails over love.

The other side of this coin is that not all that is legal is exempt from sin. For instance, our laws set virtually no limit on how much land and how many houses a person can accumulate. But Scripture clearly condemns such greed. Our laws say nothing about placing oneself ahead of all others and "looking out for number one." But Scripture clearly declares this to be sin, and a denial of the love and for-otherness for which we are created.

Nor is sin to be confused with those things for which we feel guilty. Conscience is not untainted by sin, and therefore it too does not know what sin is. Furthermore, sinful conscience is shaped by sinful society, and it too reflects the values and mores which that society seeks to impose. A feeling of guilt proves that we have done something we have been taught is evil, but that does not guarantee that it is so. Redemption is not merely the power to live according to conscience. It is also the redemption and reformation of conscience itself.

The values of our society—and indeed, of Western civilization—have twisted our understanding of sin at several points. The first of these is its "sexualization." Although theologians repeatedly tell us that sin is much more than improper sexual activity, in our common parlance "sin" is almost equated with that subject. And yet if we were to read the entire Bible, listing on the one hand the texts that seek to regulate sexual practice and on the other hand those that seek to limit and regulate property rights, we would find that the latter outweigh the former. The God of the Bible is concerned with the misuse of property at least as much as with the misuse of sex. Yet we hear very little in the church about the misuse of property. What we hear is vague, such as the notion of "stewardship." But we are not told that the "maximization of profit" is condemned by God because it violates the *rights* of the poor (see, for instance, Deut. 24:17–22; Lev. 19:9–10; 23:22). This selective preaching and teaching is not mere coincidence. Nor is it because sexual sins are more common. It is rather because we have learned to interpret "sin," like so many other elements in biblical doctrine, in a manner that is less offensive to the powerful.

Obviously, this sexualization of sin is closely connected with the hierarchical understanding of soul and body discussed in the previous section. The philosophical tradition in which that hierarchical understanding developed held that the goal of wisdom was to have the mind be totally in control of the body and its passions. Since in sexual activity the body takes control over the mind, such activity came to be seen as the opposite of the life of wisdom and virtue. When such views were introduced in the Christian church, they became one of the main impulses leading many Christians to a life of celibacy. This in turn led to a further sexualization of sin, for saints and theologians leading a celibate life and struggling against the temptations of sexual activity came to regard these as the worst temptations. And since most of those writing works on theology and spiritual treatises were men, women came to be seen as the great temptresses.

Most of these saints and theologians also had vows of poverty. Many of them had sold all their possessions and given the proceeds to the poor. Some wrote scathing remarks about greed, and about the monstrous power of runaway capital. But the church at large chose to emphasize what they had to say on the subject of sex, and to ignore their views on economic issues—except as they applied to those who, like those saints of old, had chosen the life of poverty.

The sexualization of sin is one instance of its more general "privatization." Sin has come to be seen as something between an individual and God. In the early church, the confession of sins was both public and specific. Eventually this was abandoned in favor either of private specific confession—as in Roman Catholicism—or of a public general confession—as in most Protestant churches today. The reasons for these developments were complex, and it is not necessary to discuss them here. But in any case the result was that sin came to be seen increasingly as having to do mostly with an individual's relationship to God.

Such privatization of sin contradicts the very nature of our humanity. It is "not good" for us to be alone. An individual alone is not the person God intended. We are created in for-otherness. It is only when that for-otherness takes place that we are the human beings God intends. This for-otherness is for God as well as for creation and for other human beings. We stand amid God's creation, as part of it and responsible to it and to others as the concrete expression of our responsibility toward God. As in Ortega y Gasset's famous dictum, "Yo soy yo y mi circunstancia" (I am I and my circumstance). Sin is the violation of that for-otherness. Sin is the violation of God's image in us, which is precisely the image of God's for-otherness.

The most common form sin then takes is wrongful dominance and the thirst for it. Adam names Eve, and therein lies the beginning of our societies of dominance. Wrongful sex is sinful because it denies both our own for-otherness and that of others. Joining house to house and land to land is sinful because it too denies the other's right to shelter and land. Idolatry is sinful because in it we make ourselves a god who no longer demands our for-otherness. "Dog eat dog" becomes the standard of our society. This is what Jesus would call the rule of Mammon, over against the Reign of God—and "no one can serve two masters" (Matt. 6:24).

But there is a more insidious form sin takes, particularly among women and oppressed minorities. This is to deny our for-otherness by false humility. When, in that faculty meeting I mentioned earlier, my contributions were ignored, I chose to remain silent. It would be unchristian to call their attention to what they were doing, I told myself. But the truth was that I did not wish to go through the pain and the struggle that a remark from me would have created. I excused myself on the grounds of a supposed for-otherness. I refused to stand up as "another" over against my colleagues, and in so doing I deprived them of their for-otherness toward me. I responded to their dehumanization by accepting it, at least in my dealings with them, and thus I too dehumanized them.

This is a common temptation for all oppressed groups. Many women refuse to face up to a difficult struggle by convincing themselves that they are indeed to be subservient, that to refuse to claim their own identity is a virtue. In so doing they dehumanize themselves as well as those whom they claim to love. Likewise, there are many Christian Hispanics in this country who are convinced that any form of protest, any attempt to organize in order to claim their rights, either in society or in the church, is sinful. In so doing they are accepting what those around them tell them about the nature of sin—and that in itself is wrong. And they are also dehumanizing the society in which they live by refusing to be "others," by not demanding the for-otherness of those who are in positions of power and privilege.

The usual interpretation of the passage in Genesis 3 regarding the temptation is that the serpent tempted the human creatures by declaring that they would be "like God." Seen in this light, the primal sin is pride. But as the story now stands, after the two creation narratives of Genesis 1 and 2, it would seem that the serpent was not promising them anything new. They were already "like God" (Gen. 1:26–27). Perhaps then we ought not to interpret this passage as pointing to inordinate pride—to what the Greeks called *hybris*—but rather to inordinate humility based in a lack of trust. They were already like God. They were to have dominion over all the beasts, and therefore presumably also over the serpent. And yet they refused to stand up as "others" before the tempter. In listening to the serpent and refusing to claim their godlikeness, they denied their for-otherness, just as I did when I refused to protest in that faculty meeting. The result is not only their undoing but also that of the serpent and of all creation over against which they had denied their for-otherness.

CHAPTER 10

And the Word Was Made Flesh

Although the Council of Nicea, in affirming the eternal divinity of the Word, avoided the extreme "Constantinization" of God, it did not go so far as to state that immutability is not a characteristic properly to be applied to the Christian God. On the contrary, in speaking of the "essence" (*ousia*) of God, it did imply that God could most properly be spoken of in terms of the Greek notion of substance, which is basically static. Therefore, the process begun two centuries earlier with Justin—and even before that with Philo—and of which the Trinitarian controversies were an expression, was not stopped by the Council. The political and intellectual pressures at work in the church and its theological leadership were too strong to allow them to avoid the Hellenization—and therefore the Constantinization—of God.

Such Constantinization was a relatively simple matter. After all, "No one has ever seen God." All that was necessary was to bring about a change in people's minds as to who God is. In order to do this, the Greek notion of being was readily available. By showing the "rationality" of this notion—on the basis that only the fixed and given is strictly rational—and the anthropomorphism of the images with which Scripture and early Christian theology described the living God, the exponents of the theology of the status quo were able to do away with a great deal of the biblical picture of an active, just, loving, and avenging God. At the same time, allegorical interpretation dehistoricized the Bible, and thus God's activity in history was transmuted into perennial and supposedly "higher" meanings. The pharaohs of the Roman Empire and of Western Civilization became the "new Israel," while secretly hoping that God would not upset the applecart of society, as had been done in Egypt of old.

But there was one irreducible fact that refused to be Constantinized. This fact was Jesus, the carpenter from Galilee who was called the Christ. Although "no one has ever seen God," here was one whom people had not only seen but also heard and even touched (I John 1:1). Here was a historical figure whom one must take into account.

Great pains were taken to mitigate the scandal of God's being revealed in a poor carpenter. His life and sayings were reinterpreted so as to make them more palatable to the rich and powerful. Innumerable legends were built around him, usually seeking to raise him to the level that many understood to be that of the divine—that is, to the level of a superemperor. Art depicted him as either the Almighty Ruler of the universe, sitting on his throne, or as the stolid hero who overcomes the suffering of the cross with superhuman resources and aristocratic poise.

Even after all this was said and done, there still remained the very real and very human figure of the carpenter crucified by the ruling powers, crying in his distress, and yet declared to be "very God." This was and is the stumbling block that no form of Constantinian theology can overcome.

The Attraction of Gnosticism

There are always those among the oppressed who deem it necessary to find a justification for their condition of oppression—and particularly for their subservient attitude. Freedom and dignity are always costly, as the Israelites discovered when they began missing the leeks, onions, and security of Egypt. To follow the living God means that one—an individual or an entire people—must abandon the security of all idols. It means taking the initial risk of believing in this God who is like no other god. And it means taking the further risk of challenging structures of injustice and oppression, trusting that the living God shares in the struggle. For this reason, wherever there is an oppressed group, there will be those who seek to understand their faith in such a way that their oppression and its significance will be minimized.

This was why, long before the time of Constantine, some Christians developed a theology that made it possible for them to claim faith without taking the risk faith implies for any oppressed group. This theology was gnosticism. The gnostics were well aware of the evil and injustice that abound in this world. Their solution, however, was not to oppose that evil but rather to surrender this world to the powers of evil, and to turn to a wholly different realm for their hope for meaning and vindication. According to them, original reality—and therefore also ultimate reality—was purely spiritual. The physical world is not part of a divine plan of creation but is rather the result of a mistake. In this world, and in the material bodies that are part of it, our souls are entrapped, although in truth they belong to the spiritual world. Salvation thus consists in being able to flee this material world, usually by means of a secret knowledge—hence the name "gnosticism," from the Greek *gnosis*, which means "knowledge." This secret knowledge has been brought to earth by a messenger from on high, whom Christian gnostics—there were also non-Christian gnostics—usually identified with Christ. As his message was spiritual, and this world of matter is evil, Jesus did not really come in the flesh but only appeared to do so. This view of Jesus, called docetism, had great appeal for many Christians, for it seemed to exalt Jesus by declaring him to be a purely heavenly and divine creature.

Likewise, according to the docetists, our suffering and death, as well as all the injustice and evil that exist in this world, are not important. Our bodies are prisons holding our souls in this material world and clouding our vision of spiritual realities. But when all things are consummated, our bodies and indeed all matter will be destroyed, and there will be nothing but spiritual realities.

This view of the human condition held for the dispossessed of the second and third centuries the same appeal that Egypt held for the Israelites. There is comfort in believing that whatever happens in this world has no ultimate significance, and that for that reason one is not to be too concerned about the evil one sees in the world. If the emperors and the aristocracy now live in comfort while the masses toil, or if someone owns our bodies as slaves, this is nothing to be concerned about, for in the end we shall flee from this vale of tears. If my body, or my neighbor's, is now hungry, there is little cause for concern, since bodily privations prepare the soul for its future life of freedom from the body.

These ideas were fairly common in the Hellenistic world before the advent of Christianity, and therefore the attempts to join them to the new faith were another aspect of the general adaptation of Christianity to surrounding cultures that took place during the early centuries of the life of the church. This historical assertion, however, does not contradict our thesis that the appeal of gnosticism was connected with socio-economic pressures and agendas. What took place was something similar to the process by which the philosophical notion of the Immutable One came to be equated with the God of Scripture. Gnostic ideas of salvation, like philosophical views of the One, were already playing a significant role in the world into which Christianity spread.

141

This role was not only intellectual and religious but also social and political. The role such ideas played outside of Christianity, they continued playing when joined to the new faith.

Needless to say, these views were very attractive for Christians in the second and third centuries, persecuted and oppressed as they were. A small minority, composed mostly of people from the lower classes, with no hope for redress and under constant fear of death, Christians were sorely tempted by a doctrine that promised vindication in another world and declared that present injustice was of no account. Therefore, many turned to gnosticism, even though it meant that the present evils must be endured, just as many in ancient Israel wished to return to Egypt. The great appeal of gnosticism in the first centuries of the Christian era was not, as some have thought, that it seemed to explain the mysteries of the world. Its great appeal was that it offered salvation *out* of this world, without having to confront its present evil.

Furthermore, docetism seemed to glorify Jesus by making him a purely divine being. He had none of the limitations that cause us to fret, nor was he subject to the weaknesses connected with the flesh. By saying all this, docetists seemed to be giving Jesus greater praise than did the more orthodox Christians, who insisted that Jesus was a human being, who needed to eat just as we need to eat and who was capable of suffering just as we suffer.

Gnosticism, however, was basically opposed to the witness of Scripture and to the Christian faith. Scripture taught that God made this world—this world of matter, of animals and plants—and "saw that it was good." Matter is no mistake. The material world is the result of God's loving, creative will. Therefore, matter cannot be bad. It cannot even be indifferent. Furthermore, Christians believed in a final consummation that was not purely spiritual but was rather the union of *all things* under Christ. And they believed also that part of this consummation would be the resurrection of the *flesh,* when the meek would inherit *the earth.*

The most important stumbling block gnosticism found in its way was the person of Jesus Christ. The Gospels and Christian tradition made it quite clear that he was no ethereal phantom floating in the clouds and speaking mysterious words. On the contrary, the Gospels spoke of him as being born at a particular time and place. They spoke of him as growing, eating, sleeping, weeping, perspiring, bleeding, and even dying. The Fourth Gospel affirmed that "the Word was made flesh." Indeed, the Christian message could be spoken of as that "which we have heard, which we have seen with our eyes, which we have looked upon and touched with our hands" (I John 1:1). The notion that the supreme revelation of God had taken place in such a person made it clear that spiritualist escapism was not the Christian way. Paul, for instance, had said, "He who did not spare his own Son but gave him up for us all, will he not also give us all things with him?" (Rom. 8:32). This did not mean simply that Jesus had saved Christians, and that therefore they could be certain of their salvation. It meant that God had not kept Jesus out of this world, no matter how evil, and that precisely because God had so acted, Christians knew that God's promises included "all things." Because Jesus had not escaped from the world, but had rather faced it and overcome it, Christians knew that the entire world ("all things") was their inheritance, and they were to act accordingly. Docetism, while seeming to glorify Jesus, in truth deprived him of what in the New Testament is his greatest glory: his incarnation and suffering on the cross. In the last analysis, what docetism denied was not only the reality of the incarnation and the suffering of Jesus but the very nature of a God whose greatest victory is achieved through suffering, and whose clearest revelation is in the cross.

Gnosticism, and its accompanying docetism, have always been a temptation for the oppressed. Whenever people have felt overwhelmed by their problems, or by the powers above them that control their lives and that they cannot affect, they have fled to some sort of gnosticism. This is why this heresy is so prevalent today. In our "massified" society, individuals feel lost and powerless and therefore wish to hear a "gospel" that tells them not that they are to act on the basis of the promise that "all things" are theirs but rather that they are to forget about the present life and think only of the one to come. This is the reason for the success of so many "electronic" preachers, whose message is essentially gnostic. This temptation, which has become prevalent due to the sense of lostness of the individual in today's world, is even stronger for those who belong to powerless groups. But when Hispanics succumb to the gnostic-docetic temptation, even though we may believe we are exalting Jesus, in truth, like the earlier gnostics, we are depriving him of his greatest glory. And we are also depriving ourselves of the most far-reaching consequences of his saving work, whereby we shall be given "all things" jointly with him.

The Attraction of Adoptionism

While the early church struggled with the threat and the temptation of gnostic docetism, the extreme opposite also appeared. This was adoptionism, a view that took many different shapes but that in general

143

declared that Jesus was a "mere man" who somehow had been adopted into divine sonship. The classical exponent of this position was Paul of Samosata, who lived in the third century;[1] but from an earlier time there had been others who held similar views, such as the "ebionites," whose doctrines are not well known. In any case, what all these views held was that Jesus was divine only "by adoption," and not "by nature." In the case of Paul of Samosata, the divine presence in Jesus was "impersonal" and differed from God's presence in the prophets only in degree.

It is significant that such views were not as attractive to early Christians as were those of the docetists. In fact, the early church seems to have been rid of various forms of adoptionism without great difficulty. The one great exponent of adoptionism, Paul of Samosata, did not have a wide following, and the only reason why he gained a significant hearing was that he was also a public official with a measure of power. In general, the rank and file of early Christians do not seem to have found adoptionism particularly alluring. The same is true of oppressed Christians today. Adoptionism is not a temptation for Hispanic Americans, for Afro-Americans, or for the poor in Latin America. The revival of adoptionism among liberal theologians in the nineteenth and twentieth centuries has had little effect beyond the middle class those liberals represent.[2]

The reason for this is that adoptionism is the christological expression of a myth that minorities and other oppressed groups have always known to be oppressive. This is the myth that "anyone can make it." Those who belong to the higher classes have a vested interest in this myth, for it implies that their privilege is based on their effort and achievement. But those who belong to the lower classes and who have not been propagandized into alienation from their reality know that this is a myth, and that the few that do make it are in fact allowed to move on in order to preserve the myth.

A clear example of the manner in which this myth works, and of its insensitivity to the plight of the oppressed, is the movie of the life of Jackie Robinson, released years ago. After showing all the difficulties Robinson had to overcome in order to play major league baseball, the movie ends with words to the effect that this is a story that happened in America, the country where any boy can grow up to be president, or to play for the Brooklyn Dodgers. The story itself gives the lie to that assertion, for what it shows is that this is a country where society handicaps a black child from the moment of birth. And yet, as predominantly white audiences heard those lines, they would burst into applause! What we have here is a myth so constitutive to the social life of this nation, and to the privileges of some within it, that it has to be believed even when the clear facts belie it.

The oppressed, however, must know the myth for what it is, for otherwise they must accept the conclusion that their lower status in society is the result of their lower worth. Most of those in minority communities who do accept the myth live in destructive self-deprecation and even self-hatred. A few others who believe it and do "make good" are then used as proof of the truth of the myth. But they can only do this by claiming that their success is somehow due to their superior qualities. The result is that they are alienated from the underprivileged community from which they have emerged. And the even more tragic result is that such communities are thus deprived of many of the leaders who could help them move out of their deprivation.

Adoptionism is seen as an alienating doctrine by those who realize that their society is in fact closed. One of us making it is important; but it does not end the basic structure of injustice, which is the real issue. The one who "makes it" must be more than simply another one of us, more than the proof that oppression is not all that real after all. The one who "makes it" must also be the expression of a reality beyond our closed reality. Jesus Christ must be more than the first among the redeemed, more than the local boy who makes good. He must also be the Redeemer, the power from outside who breaks into our closed reality and breaks its structures of oppression. He must be more than the "adopted son of God." He must be God adopting us as sons and daughters.

The Significance of the Chalcedonian Definition

With the rejection of both docetism and adoptionism, it was clear that Christians felt the need to affirm both the humanity and the divinity of Jesus. The central christological doctrine, which the various positions of the fourth and fifth centuries sought to express and explicate, was that in Jesus Christ, and for our salvation, the divine and the human have been joined.[3]

But there was a basic difficulty in such an assertion, a difficulty that resulted from the manner in which "divine" and "human" were understood. In effect, what the church had done in accepting the notion of God as impassible, immutable, infinite, omnipotent, and so forth, was to define God in terms of negation of all human limitations. We are finite; God is infinite. We are subject to change; God is impassible. Our power is limited; God is omnipotent. God is whatever humans are not, and vice versa. These mutually exclusive understandings of both divinity and humanity were known and defined a priori, quite apart from the incarnation. And then the question was asked, how are divinity and humanity united in Jesus? Given the definition of the terms, it was like asking for hot ice cream![4]

Thus long before the christological debates erupted late in the fourth century—with Apollinarism—the church had set the stage for that debate. It had done so by turning what would necessarily be a paradox into an outright contradiction. The inescapable paradox of the incarnation, that this particular man is also the universal God, is turned into a contradiction when the terms of the union are stated on the basis of a supposed a priori knowledge of what it means to be human and what it means to be divine.

Given such an understanding of the terms of the union, two basic roads were open. The first, taken by what scholars call Alexandrine Christology, was to insist on the reality of the union and the full divinity of Jesus, even at the expense of his humanity. In some ways, this could be seen as a further refinement of the earlier and more extreme views of the docetists, for the Alexandrines coincided with the docetists in emphasizing Jesus' work as teacher, illuminator, or messenger from God. In order to perform this task, it was necessary that he be fully divine, while his humanity could be reduced to whatever was necessary for such communication. This was why the gnostics were content with speaking of an appearance of humanity. Since that view had been rejected, the Alexandrines were more careful in their statements and affirmed that Jesus did indeed have a real body, even though some of them did not see any soteriological significance in it.

The other possible road was what scholars now call Antiochene Christology. This insisted on the full humanity of Jesus, and also on his full divinity, but feared that too close a union between the two would result in the humanity being swallowed up in the divinity. For this reason, Antiochene Christology has been characterized as "disjunctive," in contrast to its "unitive" counterpart from Alexandria.

The history of the christological controversies of the fourth and fifth centuries—and even beyond—is the history of repeated clashes between these two views, with the church refusing to follow either of them to its final consequences.

By the middle of the fourth century, both docetism and adoptionism had been rejected by the vast majority of Christians. The Arian controversy was still raging, and the anti-Arian Apollinaris of Laodicea, a representative of Alexandrine Christology, sought to respond to some of the objections of the Arians by elucidating the manner in which divinity and humanity are united in Christ. His view, simply stated, was that Jesus did indeed have a human body, but that he did not have a human "rational soul." In him, according to Apollinaris, the divine Word, the eternal Son, took the place of the human rational soul. Translating this into simple language, what this means is essentially that Jesus was physically human, but that psychologically he was purely divine. In this manner, Apollinaris sought to respond to the objection of the Arians, that the incarnation proved that the Son or Word of God was mutable. According to him, the mutable body could be joined to the immutable Son, thus preserving both the union of divinity and humanity and the immutability of the Son.

This position, however, soon drew unsurmountable objections. First of all, it contradicted the clear witness of the New Testament, that Jesus did have a human mind and did think and feel like a human being. To deny this was to come dangerously close to docetism. Second, Apollinaris's view of the incarnation in fact denied that God had been joined to a true human being. A human being is not just a body in which a mind resides but is both a body and a mind. What Apollinaris proposed was a partial incarnation. The consequence of such a partial incarnation would be a partial salvation. Indeed, if God became human so that humans could be saved, it follows that if God did not take a human soul but only a body, only our bodies are saved. As Gregory Nazianzen put it,

> If anyone has put his trust in Him as a man without a human mind, he is really bereft of mind, and quite unworthy of salvation. For that which He [the Son] has not assumed He has not healed; but that which is united to His Godhead is also saved. If only half of Adam fell, then that which Christ assumes and saves may be half also; but if the whole of his nature fell, it must be united to the whole nature of Him that was begotten, and so be saved as a whole.[5]

The result was that the Council of Constantinople, in 381, rejected the views of Apollinaris but did not offer any better solution to the central christological problem of how divinity and humanity can be united in Christ.

When we look at Apollinarism from the Hispanic vantage point, we can see that such a doctrine would undo the saving power of the Jesus in whom we believe and would reinforce attitudes that lie at the root of the oppression of Hispanics and other minorities. Apollinarism implies, as Gregory of Nazianzen pointed out, that the human mind is not in need of salvation, and that our problem lies in our bodily nature. As we have seen, such notions are used by those who control a society to claim that since they are supposedly more intellectual, they are superior. Translated into societal structures, this means that the ruling powers— the "mind"—of a society are not in need of redemption—that they are not part of the problem, for the "problem" is posed by those who perform the physical tasks the society needs for survival.

The next major controversy centered around the teachings of Nestorius, patriarch of Constantinople, who held to Antiochene Christology. Nestorius declared himself in opposition to the title *theotokos* (bearer of God) as applied to Mary, and preferred to speak of her as *christotokos* or *anthropotokos* (bearer of Christ or of the human being). What was at stake here was not Mariology but rather the fundamental christological issue of whether or not the union of divinity and humanity in Christ was such that one could speak of him as one single subject. Nestorius insisted that some things are to be said of the divinity, but that others, such as being born, must be spoken only of the humanity. Against him, the Alexandrines and many others—including Bishop Leo of Rome—insisted on the doctrine of the *communicatio idiomatum*. This is the doctrine that in the incarnation the union of divinity and humanity is such that what is predicated on one can also be predicated on the other. Nestorius sought to preserve the reality of both natures by keeping them apart—by speaking, for instance, not only of two "natures" but also of two "persons." His opponents, on the other hand, pointed out that the constant distinction between the two "natures," without a real union between the two, denied the reality of the incarnation. In the end, after long and complicated theological debates and ecclesiastical negotiations that it is not necessary to discuss here, Nestorius's position was rejected, and the doctrine of the *communicatio idiomatum* became part of christological orthodoxy at the council that was eventually declared to be the Third Ecumenical Council, gathered at Ephesus in 431. This represented the defeat of the more extreme forms of "disjunctive" Christology.

Nestorianism has never been a temptation for Hispanic Christians. The reason for this is that we feel the need to assert that the broken, oppressed, and crucified Jesus is God. A disjunction between divinity and humanity in Christ that denies this would destroy the greatest appeal of Jesus for Hispanics and other groups who must live in suffering. North Atlantic Christians have often criticized Hispanics for representing Jesus and his sufferings in gory detail. This, they claim, is a sign of a defeatist religion, or of a sadomasochistic attitude that delights in pain. But this is not the case. The suffering Christ is important to Hispanics because he is the sign that God suffers with us. An emaciated Christ is the sign that God is with those who hunger. A flagellated Christ is the sign that God is with those who must bear the stripes of an unjust society. Blood and suffering have long been the lot of the impoverished masses in Latin America. Blood and suffering are the history of Mexican-Americans in the Southwest. Nestorianism denies that God took these up. For this reason, the Nestorian Christ can never be the Lord of our devotion.

On the other hand, at the Council of Chalcedon (451) the opposite type of Christology was also found wanting. Alexandrine Christology emphasized the unity of the divine and the human to such a point that the human tended to disappear, eclipsed by the brilliance of the divine. The doctrine of Eutyches, usually called "monophysism"—that is, the doctrine of "one nature"—was rejected at Chalcedon for that reason. Although the precise teaching of Eutyches—if indeed his thought was ever precise—remains obscure, in general what he and most of his supporters held was that in the union the divinity has overwhelmed the humanity, so that now one can speak as if there were nothing in Christ but the divinity. Against such views, the rest of the church held that Jesus Christ is *homoousios*—of the same substance—not only with God but also with us. The union of divine and human in Christ must not be understood in such fashion that there are no longer in him "two natures," the divine and the human.

Monophysism had to be rejected for reasons similar to those that made gnosticism unacceptable. If in Jesus the human is swallowed up in the divine, to such a point that he no longer functions as a human being, his sufferings are sham and are not like ours. He did not bear our sufferings, and therefore we cannot find in him vindication for those who now suffer. The Crucified One must be truly crucified. The gory Hispanic Christ that so offends North Atlantic sentiments must be truly smitten, truly one of us. He must be divine, for otherwise his suffering has no power to redeem, and he must also be human, for otherwise his suffering has nothing to do with ours. And the two must be joined in such a way that his true humanity is neither destroyed nor swallowed up in his divinity.

Although the debates continued long after the Council of Chalcedon, in the monothelite and monergistic controversies of the seventh century, for all practical effects the "Definition of Faith" of Chalcedon set the parameters for what thenceforth would be considered christological orthodoxy:

> Following, then, the holy Fathers, we all with one voice teach that it should be confessed that our Lord Jesus Christ is one and the same God, the Same perfect in Godhead, the Same perfect in manhood, truly God and truly man, the Same [consisting] of a rational soul and a body;

homoousios with the Father as to his Godhead, and the same *homoousios* with us as to his manhood; in all things like unto us, sin only excepted; begotten of the Father before ages as to his Godhead, and in the last days, the Same, for us and for our salvation, of Mary the Virgin *Theotokos* as to his manhood;

One and the same Christ, Son, Lord, Only-begotten, made known in two natures [which exist] without confusion, without change, without division, without separation; the difference of the natures being in no wise taken away by reason of the union, but rather the properties of each being preserved, and [both] concurring into one Person and one *hypostasis*—not parted or divided into two persons, but one and the same Son and Only-begotten, the divine Logos, the Lord Jesus Christ; even as the prophets from of old [have spoken] concerning him, and as the Lord Jesus Christ himself has taught us, and as the Symbol of the Fathers has delivered to us.[6]

This formula, which may well appear to the modern reader as little more than doubletalk, does however have some positive values, as well as some very significant shortcomings. Its greatest value is that it does indeed avoid the most serious pitfalls of both the Alexandrine and the Antiochene Christologies. Against the extreme Alexandrines, it refuses to allow the divinity in Christ to overwhelm the humanity. Against the extreme Antiochenes, it refuses to preserve the humanity of Christ by weakening or denying its union with the divine. Even though its language is unfamiliar—and perhaps even meaningless—to us, it does assert that in Jesus Christ the divine and the human were united for our salvation, and it rejects any view that diminishes the humanity, the divinity, or the union itself.

On the negative side, however, one must point out that the entire controversy, and therefore also its result in the "Definition" of Chalcedon, was posed in static terms. When this formula speaks of "humanity," we are not led to think of a child growing up (Luke 2:52) or of a young man having to make difficult decisions (Mark 1:12 and parallels). Likewise, when the formula speaks of the divine nature, we are not led to think of the active God of Scripture. In both cases, humanity and divinity are depicted as static essences. This is untrue both to the biblical witness regarding the nature of God and to the human experience of what it means to be human.

But the main shortcoming of this formula—and of the long series of controversies that led to it—is that it forgets the basic principle that we do not know who God is, nor what it means to be fully human, apart from divine revelation. We must not approach divine revelation with a preconceived notion of God and accept in that revelation only that which agrees with such a notion. In the Older Testament we have the revelation of who God is—or, more precisely, of how God acts—as well as of what it means to be human. This revelation, Christians hold, comes to its culmination in the person of Jesus Christ, in whom the God of the Older Testament is most fully revealed, and in whom the true meaning of full humanity is also revealed. Therefore, we must not approach the person of Jesus Christ with an a priori notion of what it means to be divine—in this case drawn mostly from the Greek metaphysical tradition—or with an a priori notion of what it means to be human. The proper starting point for Christology is neither theology nor anthropology—nor a combination of the two—but Jesus himself as Scripture witnesses to him.

As Karl Barth has said,

> We may believe that God can and may be absolute in contrast to all that is relative, exalted in contrast to all that is lowly, active in contrast to all suffering, inviolable in contrast to all temptation, transcendent in contrast to all immanence, and therefore divine in contrast to everything human, in short that He can and must be only the "Wholly Other." But such beliefs are shown to be quite untenable, and corrupt and pagan, by the fact that God does in fact be and do this in Jesus Christ.[7]

The One for Others

As we read the story of Jesus in the Gospels, the first thing that strikes us is that he is entirely for others. At his birth, the angel announces to the shepherds that "*to you* is born this day in the city of David a Savior" (Luke 2:11). One of the Gospel texts most often quoted (and seldom pondered) declares that "God so loved the world that he *gave* . . ." (John 3:16). The cross, toward which the entire gospel narrative moves, is not an accident but the result of Jesus' active giving up of his life: "For this reason the Father loves me, because I lay down my life, that I may take it again. No one takes it from me, but I lay it down of my own accord" (John 10:17–18). At the cross itself, Jesus is still the One for others, praying, "Father, forgive them; for they know not what they do" (Luke 23:34). Even his return to the Father, which in a sense is the seal of his victory, is for others: "I go to prepare a place for you" (John 14:2).

Nor was this the easy self-deprecation whereby we often hide cowardice behind humility. His was a strong, assertive "for-otherness." He was for others, not only when he healed the sick, forgave those who condemned him, and died on the cross but also when he cleansed the Temple, spoke the harsh truth to the Pharisees, and called Herod a fox.

He proclaimed that in the new order he had come to usher in, the greatest would be the one who served, and he lived out his proclamation by being the greatest servant of all. He entered Jerusalem astride the colt of an ass—a sign of humility, but also a claim that he was the ruler promised by the prophet (Matt. 21:5; Zech. 9:9). When some friendly Pharisees warned him that Herod was plotting to kill him, he responded by insisting on his own timetable: "Behold, I cast out demons and perform cures today and tomorrow, and the third day I finish my course" (Luke 13:32). The for-otherness of Jesus is such that his lordship consists precisely in it. As Barth has said, "What a Lord among a race of servants was this perfect servant in His very being as a servant!"[8]

Since the present order of the world is not one of equality, his stern for-otherness was not evenhanded. He could break all social proprieties by speaking to a Samaritan adulteress (John 4:9) and could be harsh with the socially acceptable and profoundly religious Pharisees and scribes. He would pronounce blessing and curse almost in the same breath, and this not on the basis of religious practice but on the place of different people in the ordering of society:

> Blessed are you poor, for yours is the kingdom of God.
> Blessed are you that hunger now, for you shall be satisfied.
> Blessed are you that weep now, for you shall laugh.
> Blessed are you when men hate you, and when they exclude you and revile you, and cast out your name as evil, on account of the Son of Man! Rejoice in that day, and leap for joy, for behold, your reward is great in heaven; for so their fathers did to the prophets.
> But woe to you that are rich, for you have received your consolation.
> Woe to you that are full now, for you shall hunger.
> Woe to you that laugh now, for you shall mourn and weep.
> Woe to you, when all men speak well of you, for so their fathers did to the false prophets. (Luke 6:20–26)

Did all this make him more human, or more divine? To pose the question thus is again to miss the central point of the incarnation. Divine and human are not two opposite poles, like red and violet in the spectrum, so that as one approaches one pole one moves away from the other. Being more human does not make Jesus less divine. And being more divine does not make him less human. Actually, it is precisely in his being for others that Jesus manifests his full divinity, and it is also in his being for others that he manifests his full humanity.

God is being-for-others. This is what is meant by the central biblical affirmation that "God is love" (I John 4:8). To love is to be for others. That is also, as was shown in chapter 7, why the doctrine of the Trinity is essential to a Christian understanding of God: "God is love" means first of all that God loves Godself within the divine Trinity. But "God is love" also means that God is being-for-the-world. "God so loved the world," says the Fourth Gospel. Creation, preservation, judgment, redemption, and consummation are acts of God's love, of God's being-for-others. The God who gave Godself in Jesus is none other than the God who in creation gave up existence in solitary splendor, who in Abraham loved a wandering Aramean, and who in the Exodus loved an enslaved people.

This divine for-otherness, however, is not the easy self-deprecation of those who hide behind humility to avoid pain and difficulty. It is a sovereign for-otherness, which includes not only forgiveness and redemption but also judgment and condemnation. God's love does not work in equal fashion for all individuals and peoples, because individuals and peoples do not relate to each other as equals. Hence God's preferential care for the poor, the widow, the alien, and the oppressed, all of whom enjoy special protection in the Law, and for whom the prophets repeatedly demanded justice. When God acts, as Mary declares at the beginning of the Gospel,

> He has shown strength with his arm,
>> he has scattered the proud in the imagination of their hearts,
>> he has put down the mighty from their thrones,
> and exalted those of low degree;
>> he has filled the hungry with good things,
> and the rich he has sent empty away. (Luke 1:51–53)

God's for-otherness is such that this is the reason why the world and humankind were made. Commenting on those who claim to understand in order not to be awed, Miguel de Unamuno wrote: "They have gone so far ask to ask stupidly why God made the world, and they have replied, 'for his glory!' And this has made them so proud and satisfied as if the bores knew what is this business of the glory of God."[9] But the truth is that we do know what the glory of God is. The glory of God is what the Israelites saw in the Exodus: God's acts on behalf of the oppressed children of Israel (Num. 14:22).

This for-otherness that is the glory of God is also the glory of Jesus Christ. John 1:14 declares that "the Word became flesh" and that "we have beheld his glory, glory as of the only Son from the Father." Some have interpreted this to mean that the Fourth Gospel espouses a semi-gnostic view of Jesus, so that his "glory," almost like a halo, could be seen in him. This is not what the text means. The glory of Jesus is like the glory of God. The glory of Jesus is the very glory that the Israelites beheld in the opening of the sea. The glory of Jesus is the same as the glory of God: for-otherness, love.

Thus the full divinity of Jesus is seen in his judging, redeeming, self-giving love. But, oddly enough, it is also that very love that reveals his full humanity.

Christ the Source of New Life

All of this, however, is important not as an explanation of the incarnation but in determining who we are and what Christ does for us. It is not a matter of speculation about the meaning of "divinity" and "humanity." It is rather the existential and urgent matter of what it means for us to be human, and how we can get on with the business of being human in the midst of an oppressive society.

Ever since the publication of Gustav Aulén's *Christus Victor*,[10] it has become a commonplace that the "classic" understanding of the work of Christ is one in which he conquers the powers of evil and makes us participants of his victory by uniting us to him. The other two options Aulén discussed, neither of which is as ancient as the "classical" one, are, first, the view that the human problem is that we owe a debt to God and that Christ comes to pay that debt, and, second, that our problem is that we lack knowledge or inspiration to love God and that Christ therefore comes to show us the way by his example.

What has not usually been pointed out is that these various views are related to sociopolitical issues and situations.[11] The juridical view that makes us debtors before God is very suited to keeping people in their place. In its most extreme forms, it appears together with phrases such as "we are nothing but worms" or "there is no good in us." The so-called "subjective" view, which makes Jesus an example or teacher, implies that our only problem is that we do not know enough or are not sufficiently moved to love and serve God. This is particularly attractive to the middle-class ethos that we are what we make ourselves to be, and that success in life is essentially the result of hard work and clean living. Over against these understandings, the "classical" view is particularly relevant to those who realize that the core of the human predicament is neither a debt to God nor a lack of spirituality but an enslavement to powers of evil. This was true of the early church, and it is no coincidence that the "classical" view of atonement began receding into the background when the church became powerful. It is also true of Hispanics and others who repeatedly discover that there are powers and structures that stand in the way of their full humanity. Therefore, among such

Christians the "classical" theory of atonement, often set aside as too crass by other Christians—fundamentalists as well as liberals—becomes central to an understanding of the work of Christ. This is not to say that the Anselmian view of the Atonement as payment to God for our sin is not still prevalent among Hispanics. Indeed, such a view is practically the summary of the Gospel as we have heard it both from traditional Roman Catholic teaching and from Protestant missionaries. What is clear, however, is that when Hispanics hear of the work of Christ as the One who conquers sin and frees us from its bondage, they avidly incorporate this into their theology and devotion.

Another ancient theme in Christian theology is that God became human so that humans could become divine.[12] Western theologians have often found fault with this statement, declaring that it tends to erase the distance between the divine and the human—and in that very declaration forgetting that this is precisely what has happened in the incarnation. They have also tended to speak of this view as radically different from the "classical" one, even though the exponents of one are often the exponents of the other. But at this point such theologians forget that the divine intention at the very act of creation is that we be Godlike. The task of theology is *not* to preserve the divinity of God by devaluing the human creature. It would be a very petty God whose divinity must be exalted by such means. In any case, where such critics of early Christian theology err is in thinking in static, metaphysical terms. What was meant by the above-quoted phrase was not that humans were to become "divine" in a metaphysical sense but rather that they were to grow into closer communion with God, and thus become more like God. God's very being is love, for-otherness. This is the Trinitarian God. This is the God revealed in Jesus Christ. What Jesus has done is precisely to open for us the way of love, to free us so that we too can begin to be for others. In being for others we are most truly human. And in being most truly human we are most Godlike. Indeed, God did become human so that we could become divine!

CHAPTER 11

Life in the Spirit

There is a general malaise in the air around Protestantism. Mainline churches, painfully aware of uninspiring statistics, eagerly grope for explanations and solutions. Most of what one hears are easy prescriptions, as if the malaise had to do essentially with structural matters that some program or constitutional revision could fix.[1] Such prescriptions are attractive, for they require of us no more than some tinkering with our organization, or some new program that could be launched by means of budgetary adjustments. But the problem is much deeper than that. The problem really has to do with the meaning of the gospel and how we apply it, not only in our individual lives but also in the communal and structural life of the church. It is for this reason that "spirituality" has become such an important subject. The term, of ancient and common usage in the Roman Catholic tradition, has gained new currency in mainline Protestantism. Properly understood, spirituality has to do with the manner in which the gospel is both "lived in" and "lived out." Spirituality is first of all living *in* the gospel—making faith the foundation for life. And it is also living *out* the gospel—making faith the foundation of action and structure. Therefore, the solution to our present malaise will not be found until we deal with issues of spirituality and come to a spirituality that is both deeply grounded in Scripture and radically relevant to today's world.

Spirituality and the Spirit of *Mañana*

On this subject, the first point to be noted is that Christian spirituality is not based on the distinction between spirit and matter. Indeed, such a distinction, if it appears in Scripture at all, is a very secondary theme. Were we to say, as many take for granted, that such a distinction is the fundamental presupposition of Christian spirituality, and were we then to read Scripture in quest for guidance, we would be hard pressed. In the entire canon of Scripture there are not more than a few texts that could be cited as support for contrasting matter and spirit, and even these are subject to other interpretations.

What has happened, as historians and Bible scholars know, is that during the early centuries of Christian history the contrast between matter and spirit, which was commonplace in Hellenistic religiosity, found its way into Christian theology and piety, to the point that later generations came to think that such a contrast was the mainstay of Christian spirituality.

Whether or not there are indeed those two realities, and how they may differ, is not the point here. The point is that such a distinction is not at the very core of the biblical understanding of reality and should not therefore be construed as the centerpiece of Christian spirituality.

The basis for Christian spirituality is not "the spiritual" in the sense of the nonmaterial. The basis for Christian spirituality is the Spirit—the Holy Spirit of God. Therefore, in biblical parlance one is "spiritual" not because one is primarily concerned with "spiritual" things in contrast to the "material" but because of the presence of the Holy Spirit. A "spiritual" person is not one who flexes and develops his or her spirit, as an athlete flexes and develops muscles, but one in whom the Spirit of the Lord dwells. This is the first basic point that we must keep in mind as we search for the biblical meaning of "spirituality."

Were Isaiah and Micah "spiritual"? If by that we mean were they concerned about the survival of their souls after death, and did they set aside material concerns in favor of those "beyond," the answer is clearly no. The same would be the case of all the great figures of the Older Testament. If it is true, as was said earlier, that we must not only interpret the Older Testament in the light of the New but also the New in the light of the Older, this means that whatever we say about the central message of Scripture—and about the nature of spirituality—must show the continuity between the two Testaments. To say, therefore, that the central message of Scripture is "spiritual" in the sense of being otherworldly is to deny the authority of the Older Testament, and to fall into a veiled sort of Marcionism.

The second basic point is that when the Bible contrasts the spiritual with its opposite, that other pole is not the "material" but the "old" or—even more surprisingly—the "soulish." Let us look at those two contrasts as they appear in the Pauline literature.

First of all, there is the contrast between the spiritual/new and the old. In Paul, this has to do with the reality of being crucified with Christ and raised with him. This reality is not, as some have thought, the culmination of Christian life but its very beginning and foundation. One does not become a Christian and then, through hard work and a process of renunciation, die with Christ. The very act of becoming a Christian, of being born anew, is an act of dying to the old.[2] All the rest is simply living out what we already are. Paul puts this very clearly in Colossians 3:3–4: "For you have died, and your life is hid with Christ in God. When Christ who is our life appears, then you also will appear with him in glory." Elsewhere, Paul declares that "our old self was crucified with him so that the sinful body might be destroyed, and we might no longer be enslaved to sin" (Rom. 6:6) and, in a passage often quoted but seldom understood in all of its radical implications, "if any one is in Christ, he is a new creation; the old has passed away, behold, the new has come" (II Cor. 5:17). Part of the reason why we miss the radicality of this text is that the structure of the English language makes it difficult to translate it more directly. Perhaps a more literal translation would read, "If any one is in Christ, new creation! The old has passed away! Behold, the new has come!" The difference is that while the usual translation implies that it is the Christian who is made a new creation, what the Greek actually says is that all things are renewed—indeed, some ancient manuscripts add the word "everything" and thus read "everything is a new creation." In any case, in the light of these passages and many more, is should be clear that the contrast between the old and the new stands at the very foundation of Christian life and spirituality, and that this newness is such that it does not simply stem from the old, as its natural outcome and development, but is rather the result of a divine intervention.

The other term that Paul opposes to "spiritual" is, surprisingly enough, "soulish." Since such a word does not exist in English, when Paul uses it our modern translations employ another. In I Corinthians 2:14, for instance, the Revised Standard Version and the Jerusalem Bible translate it as "unspiritual," while the New American Standard Bible says "natural." The difficulty in translating this word is shown in that most of the versions that say "natural" include a footnote suggesting the alternative translation "unspiritual," and those that say "unspiritual" often have a footnote suggesting the alternative translation "natural." What the Greek actually says is "soulish," and therefore the contrast in I Corinthians 2:14–15 is between the "soulish" person and the "spiritual." Either translation, "unspiritual" or "natural," is correct, as long as we understand what is meant. Essentially, the meaning is that without the Spirit of God, there is no spirituality. By their nature, human beings are "soulish." Even the most "unspiritual" have a life of the soul.

But this should not be confused with that spiritual life which is the result of the Holy Spirit. Without such Spirit, we are "unspiritual," "natural," or "soulish." By nature, we have a life beyond the merely material, but even that life is unspiritual.

Therefore, the contrast that is absolutely essential in order to understand the biblical notion of spirituality is that between Spirit and nature. "Nature" in this context is not exactly what we mean when we speak, for instance, of natural phenomena or of the laws of nature. Nature, in the sense of the created cosmos, is the work of God—indeed, in that sense nature is a spiritual creation, for Genesis 1:2 says that "the Spirit of God was moving over the face of the waters." All things that God has made God has made through the Spirit. All things that God now does, God does through the Spirit. All things that God will do, God will do through the Spirit. In this sense, all created reality is the result of the work of the Spirit and has a spiritual dimension. It is not in this sense that Scripture contrasts the "natural" and the "spiritual."

The word "nature," however, has another meaning. In this other sense, "nature" is that impulse in things that makes them be what they are and act as they do. It is the nature of a fire to burn. It is the nature of the sun to shine. And, because we are all part of a fallen creation and therefore subject to sin, it is the nature of humans to sin.

From this perspective, we can see that what characterizes "nature" in contrast with "Spirit" is that nature is a given. While nature is the inner force that makes things be what they are, the Spirit is the power that intervenes to make things become what they are not. Through the power of the Spirit, the world is created out of the void. Through the power of the same Spirit, the "natural human being"—the "old," "soulish," "unspiritual" human being—is created anew, so that sinful nature no longer holds sway.

In this sense, nature is the past, the old, the given, while Spirit is the power of the future, the new, the promised. It is on this basis that, a few verses before the passage on the "soulish" and the "spiritual," Paul contrasts the "spirit of the world" with the "Spirit of God": "Now we have received not the spirit of the world, but the Spirit which is from God, that we might understand the gifts bestowed on us by God" (I Cor. 2:12). That is to say, the spirit of the world only sees the "natural," that which is before its eyes or that which naturally follows from the present order, while the Spirit of God allows us to see "what has been bestowed to us," the coming Reign, the new order, our inheritance, the promise.

The Spirit of God is the guarantor of what has been granted to us—granted with that "not yet" and that "already" which are always the character of a promise. The Spirit is the firstfruits, the down payment, of the Reign (Rom. 8:23). And this Reign, according to Scripture, is not purely "spiritual" in the common sense of the word but is rather a Reign in which some are promised "the earth" as their inheritance and others that their "hunger and thirst after justice" will be satisfied.

Those, therefore, who insist that Christian spirituality is different from the "spirit of the world" are correct. Where they often err is in thinking that rejecting the "spirit of the world" somehow involves rejecting matter, or leaving aside those concerns that have to do with material things.

The Spirit of God is the firstfruits, the down payment, the guarantor, of the Reign of God. Before we go much further, however, we must pause to consider what is meant by that phrase, "the Reign (or, in more traditional language, the Kingdom) of God." Clearly, to speak of the Reign of God implies that there is at present another reign, another order, that is under "the ruler of this world" (John 12:31; 14:30; 16:11). The present order is not that which has been promised by God. We still await the Reign of which the Spirit is the firstfruits.

Yet the contrast between these two has often been misconstrued in ways that are not only oppressive, but also unbiblical. Therefore, it is important to remember that this contrast is temporal rather than spatial, and structural rather than ontological.

The spatial image of the contrast between the two reigns leads us to think in terms of a reign whose primary locus is this physical earth, and another Reign of God to be found elsewhere, in a "beyond." Yet the contrast Scripture most often depicts between these two reigns is temporal: It has to do with "the last days," with "those days," with "the day of the Lord." The reign for which we long and pray ("thy Kingdom come") is not "up there" but "out ahead." The distance between us and the Reign is best described not as that between "here" and "there" but rather as that between "now" and "then."

This understanding of the message of Scripture provides continuity between the two Testaments. All of the Older Testament is pressing forward toward God's "then"—or, as the prophets call it, "the Day of the Lord." The God of the Older Testament is the One who does and promises to do "new things." This is true both at the individual and at the corporate level. At the individual level, for instance, the Psalmist can say "put a new and right spirit within me" (Ps. 51:10). At the corporate, the height of praise is singing a "new song" to the Lord, not simply as an expression of artistic creativity but also as a response to the new things that God does. In Isaiah 42:10, for instance, the people are called to "sing to the Lord a new song," and as the words of the

161

prophet unfold we are told that the reason for such a new song is that God says,

> Behold, I am doing a new thing;
>   now it springs forth, do you not perceive it?
> I will make a way in the wilderness
>   and rivers in the desert. (Isaiah 43:19).[3]

From this perspective, the gift of the Spirit is an "already," a "finally." As Peter says to his hearers at Pentecost, "This is what was spoken by the prophet Joel: 'And in the last days . . . ' " (Acts 2:16–17).

The contrast is structural rather than ontological. When we hear of "two reigns," we often think that some things belong to this reign and others to the other. There have been periods in the history of the church, for instance, when people have spoken in terms of one reign over bodies and another reign over souls. Some have even said that the gospel is to govern over one of these spheres and the civil government over the other.[4] However, the contrast between the present reign and the one to come is not based on the ontological nature of things—that some are physical and others spiritual. The contrast is based rather in the order and the structure that prevail in each of these two reigns. In one of them the powerful rule, all seek their own profit, and those whom no one defends are oppressed. In the other, God rules, and therefore love rules. What characterizes the Reign of God is not that it is in a different place, nor that it involves different realities, but that it is a Reign of love.

Such a Reign is not "of this world" (John 18:36), not because it involves different realities or different places but because it involves a different order. As Jesus himself said,

> You know that those who are supposed to rule over the Gentiles lord it over them, and their great men exercise authority over them. But it shall not be so among you; but whoever would be great among you must be your servant, and whoever would be first among you must be slave of all. For the Son of man came not to be served but to serve, and to give his life as a ransom for many. (Mark 10:42–45 and parallels)

If one thing is clear in the early chapters of Acts, it is precisely that part of the function of the Spirit is to allow the believing community to live already, at least partially, in the "not yet" of the Reign. The quotation from Joel in Acts 2 plays the same role in the entire book that the quotation from Isaiah plays in Luke 4. Both are an announcement of the mission of the main protagonist of the book—Jesus in Luke and the Spirit in Acts. What the quotation from Joel says is that the Spirit is poured out on "all flesh" and that this includes the young and the old, sons and daughters, and even slaves, both male and female (Acts 2:17–

18). The rest of the book—at least, in its early chapters—is the unfolding of this action of the Spirit. What happens in those early chapters is that the church slowly discovers what life in the Spirit means: breaking bread, witnessing, sharing possessions, reaching out to the Gentiles, and so forth. The early church is spiritual not because it spends all its time in prayer and meditation but because it is a church seeking to live out of the future that the Spirit makes present.

On this basis, being "spiritual" means living out of the future we have been promised, precisely because that promise has been sealed and guaranteed by the Holy Spirit. What this means is that Christian spirituality—that genuinely Christian spirituality that is based not on our own "spiritual" or "soulish" powers but on the presence of the Holy Spirit—is eschatological in nature. It is future oriented. It is life lived out of an expectation, out of a hope and a goal. And that goal is the coming Reign of God. To have the Spirit is to have a foot up on the stirrup of the eschatological future and to live now as those who expect a new reality, the coming of the Reign of God.

An example will illustrate the implications of such future-oriented living and witness. If I say that I hope someday to move to Japan and to spend the rest of my days in Japan, for I am convinced that no culture is as enlightened, no art as beautiful, no literature as meaningful, as that of Japan, the depth of my conviction will be judged by my present actions. If I am thoroughly convinced that what I say is true, I will begin studying Japanese. If, on the other hand, I start building a dream house in which to retire in Georgia and devote my time to studying Italian, all my enthusiastic declarations about my devotion to Japanese culture and Japanese ways will sound hollow. If I truly believe what I say about Japan, I will certainly begin practicing Japanese, and I will begin looking at my present-day life under a new light.

The same is true of the expectation of the Reign of God. So long as we proclaim the Reign but make little effort to speak even a few words of "Reignese," our witness will hardly be credible. If, by the power of the Spirit, we are a pilgrim people looking forward to the coming Reign of God, we had better begin practicing the love of that Reign—we had better begin organizing our lives according to the new order that we know is coming and that we proclaim.

This is one of the reasons why it is so difficult for the rich to enter the Kingdom (Matt. 19:24). One's investments in the present order make it very difficult to live in eager expectation of a different order—just as my dream house in Georgia would make it more difficult and unlikely that I would move to Japan.

163

The Church as *Mañana* People

This is also the reason why eschatological expectation is so real in many Hispanic churches. When people in the dominant culture wish to make fun of us and to imply that we are lazy folk who never get anything done, they employ one of the few Spanish words they have ever bothered to learn: *Mañana*. From their perspective, *mañana* is the indolent response of people too lazy to make any kind of effort. The truth of the matter, however, is much more complex. *Mañana* is most often the discouraged response of those who have learned, through long and bitter experience, that the results of their efforts seldom bring about much benefit to them or to their loved ones. In this sense, *mañana* is the response of farm workers who realize that no matter how hard they work, most of their income will end up back in the hands of the employer; or of the tenement dweller in New York who knows that efforts to improve living conditions will most likely be erased by slum lords, drug traffickers, and even city ordinances.

There is, however, another dimension of *mañana*. *Mañana* is much more than "tomorrow." It is the radical questioning of today. For those who control the present order of society, today is the time to build for tomorrow, and tomorrow will bring about the fruits of what they sow today. For impoverished Hispanics and others, the real *mañana* is a time unlike today. It is a time of a new reality, not the outcome of today's disorderly order but the outcome of other factors that bring about a breach with an unbearable today. For some Hispanics, the only hope of such a break between today and *mañana* is "pegarse el gordo"—hitting the jackpot. And so they gamble. For others, the break comes through drugs, which promise release, no matter how brief, from a hopeless today.

Then there are those who capture the *mañana* vision of Scripture. The world will not always be as it is. It will not even be an outgrowth of what is. God who created the world in the first place is about to do a new thing—a thing as great and as surprising as that first act of creation. God is already doing this new thing, and we can join it by the power of the Spirit! *Mañana* is here! True, *mañana* is not yet today, but today can be lived out of the glory and the promise of *mañana*, thanks to the power of the Spirit.

Mañana, however, is also a word of judgment on today. When one looks forward to a *mañana*, one implies that the present is not as rosy as some would have us think. It is no coincidence that almost immediately after Constantine's conversion, there were many who felt that the book of Revelation ought not to be included in the canon. Not only did it speak of Rome—and Rome was now Christian—as the harlot sitting on seven hills and drunk with the blood of the martyrs, but it also spoke of a new heaven and a new earth, thereby implying that the "benevolent" reign of the emperor was far distant from the Reign of God.

The same is true today, although at a more subtle level. "Enlightened" theologians, followed by equally "enlightened" Christians, look down on any but the most idealized eschatological expectation. Among "sophisticated" Christians, it is common to speak of a vivid eschatological expectation as unsophisticated, and to make fun of it. At the theological level, liberal theologians tell us that eschatological expectation undercuts the social and political action of Christians. However, this is true only on the basis of a particular understanding of eschatology or of a particular understanding of social and political action.

It is true that a certain understanding of eschatology discourages action in the social sphere. The "spiritualist" eschatology that is so often proclaimed over radio and television certainly undercuts any understanding of Christian responsibility that would lead believers to engage in social or political action. The reason, however, is not that it is eschatological; the reason is rather that it is falsely spiritual. Quite clearly, anyone who believes that the future that God promises has nothing to do with physical life and with the social order will hardly be overly interested in the political struggles of our day.

Yet this is not the only understanding of eschatology. There are other views that make eschatology the driving force for drastic political action. The many revolutionary movements inspired by eschatology that cover the pages of church history are ample proof of this. Indeed, the great rebellions of the Middle Ages, as well as those of the Anabaptists in the sixteenth century, were based on a vivid eschatological expectation. And even though it is true that "pie in the sky" was a message intended to keep slaves in a position of subservience, it is also true that eschatological expectation has played an important role in the Afro-American struggle for liberation. In the first place, "pie in the sky" led many to question, How come there will be pie in the sky and nothing but greens and sweat on earth? If God's intended order is that we have pie, how come others get all the pies and we get all the pain? And in the second place, the promise of a final, inalienable victory made the movement unstoppable, for there is nothing a master can to do suppress the freedom of one who sings, "Oh freedom, oh freedom over me; and before I'd be a slave I'll be buried in my grave and go home to my Lord and be free."

Nor is the liberal understanding of social and political action the only option. One must recall that theological liberalism was born during the heyday of bourgeois economic liberalism, and that in many ways it reflects its values. Just as economic liberalism (which now, through a strange quirk in the evolution of language, is called "conservatism" in the United States) was predicated on the theory that wealth was the reward of work and wits, and that the few who deserve economic success will achieve it, so is theological liberalism content with a social and political action that makes it possible for a few more to achieve success. There is, however, another sort of political and social action—one that seeks not merely the evolution of today into tomorrow but rather the breach that *mañana* announces. This is the practice of the prophets. This is also the manner in which the early church is politically active. It is a small group of insignificant people, and yet their activity soon brings upon them the wrath of the mighty Roman Empire. Why? Because by their mere existence, by their living out of *mañana*, they question the very foundations of the Roman social order.

There are many images of the church in the New Testament. It is significant, however, that when these images are understood in the context of the piety of the dominant culture, they tend to be static and present oriented, when in fact much of their original meaning is dynamic and future oriented. The church is the body of Christ, we are told, and for many of us this means that "he has no hands but our hands." This is not only a misinterpretation of the image but also blasphemy! The Lord may wish to use us as hands, but were we to fail, there is no doubt that the Lord would find other hands to carry forth the divine purposes. To be the body of Christ means to share in his life. The way the early church understood it was that just as Christ our head has arisen, so too will we arise; and now, while we wait for the final consummation, we have new life by being grafted into the body of the True Life.[5] To be the body of Christ means to derive our life from the ruler of the coming order, and thus to live now as "priests and kings" (I Pet. 2:9; Rev. 1:6, 5:10). Those who today already benefit from power, respect, and prestige can hardly understand the enormous significance of this new reality for those whose daily lot is suffering, poverty, and humiliation, and who are now told that in the order of *mañana*, which in a sense is already here, they are "a chosen race, a royal priesthood, a holy nation."

For Hispanics, the church is a pilgrim people, but a people whose pilgrimage is no uncertain wandering. It is a pilgrimage to a *mañana* made possible by the death and resurrection of Jesus Christ, made

166

present by the Spirit, and made certain by the power and the promise of none other than God Almighty!

The Good News of *Mañana*

It is at this point that the entire debate about whether we should emphasize "justice" or "evangelism" collapses, and at the same time becomes much wider. The question is not whether we should emphasize one or the other. Nor is the question one of strategy. The question is rather whether we are willing to live out of that spirituality which, by the presence of the Holy Spirit, makes us the people of the Reign of God.

This is the basic flaw in most of our contemporary schemes for evangelism and church growth. We try to bring the church out of its spiritual malaise not by grounding our solutions on the Spirit who is the firstfruits of the Reign but by borrowing some marketing or organizational scheme on which we then put our faith. It was said above that if we truly believe that our future is in the Reign of God, we shall start practicing "Reignese" right now, just as one who believes that the future is in Japan will start practicing Japanese. The problem with many of our proposed solutions to the present malaise about evangelism and lack of church growth is that instead of trying to develop practices and structures on the basis of the grammar of Reignese, we try to emulate "successful" organizations of "this world," and to apply their grammar. Some years ago it was "management by objectives." Now we are told that what we need is a chief executive officer. The fact is that we have had a Chief Executive Officer for all these centuries and have not been very good at following him! Perhaps having an administrative head will help, perhaps not; but it is unlikely that it will do much to make us more faithful!

At the very heart of evangelism stands the good news that through the sacrifice and resurrection of Jesus Christ, God's Reign is coming and is now open to us. By the power and presence of the Spirit, we can live now as citizens of the coming city, as subjects of the One whose Reign will have no end. But our witness to the good news is credible only insofar as we too live as those who believe the message and are willing to stake our lives on it. To love the neighbor, to do justice, to announce peace, to care for the widow and the orphan—all these are not things we do beyond or apart from proclaiming the good news. They are a necessary part of the good news. Evangelism must be grounded on the spirituality of the Reign of God or it is not the good news of Jesus Christ.

167

NOTES

Chapter 1

1. *Attack upon Christendom:* 1854–1855 (Boston: Beacon Press, 1944), p. 181.

2. "I moved on to other things, including a dramatic/traumatic change of consciousness from 'radical Catholic' to post-Christian feminist." Mary Daly, *The Church and the Second Sex,* 2nd ed. (New York: Harper Colophon Books, 1975), p. 5.

3. "Christian doctrines and beliefs and some of the beliefs of Indian tribal groups, which appear to stand in direct opposition. The opposition is more than merely conceptual; it colors the manner in which non-Indians view the world and the people they deal with in that world, particularly Indians." Vine Deloria, Jr., *God Is Red* (New York: Dell, 1973), p. 289.

4. "Once I was a Catholic. I was baptized, made my first Communion, my Confirmation, and I wore a Cross with Jesus on it around my neck. I prayed at night, said my Rosary, went to Confession, and said all the Hail Marys and Our Fathers to which I was sentenced by the priest. . . . I chose the Catholic Church because all the Negroes and Mexicans went there. The whites went to the Protestant chapel. Had I been fool enough to go to the Protestant chapel, one black face in a sea of white, and with guerrilla warfare going on between us, I might have ended up a Christian martyr—St. Eldridge the Stupe." Eldridge Cleaver, *Soul on Ice* (New York: Dell, 1968), p. 30.

5. "The Christian religion is incompatible with the Negro's aspirations for dignity and equality in America. It has hindered where it might have helped; it has been evasive when it was morally bound to be forthright; it has separated believers on the basis of color although it has declared its mission to be a universal brotherhood under Jesus Christ. Christian love is the white man's love for himself and for his race. For the man who is not white, Islam is the hope for justice and equality in the world we must build tomorrow." A student at Clark College in 1956, quoted by C. Eric Lincoln, *The Black Muslims in America* (Boston: Beacon Press, 1961), p. iii.

6. Probably the best known of these, among dozens, are Marabel Morgan, *The Total Woman* (Old Tappan, N.J.: Fleming H. Revell, 1973), and Helen B. Andelin, *Fascinating Womanhood* (Santa Barbara, Calif.: Pacific Press, 1965). In

169

1975, at the request of the Committee on Women's Concerns of the Presbyterian Church (U.S.), my wife and I wrote a theological critique of these books: "How Total is 'Total'?"

7. As examples of how women have undertaken this task, see Rachel C. Wahlberg, *Jesus According to a Woman* (New York: Paulist Press, 1975), and Letty M. Russell, ed., *Feminist Interpretation of the Bible* (Philadelphia: Westminster Press, 1985).

8. The documents illustrating this trend are many. The turning point was clearly the Second Conference of Latin American Bishops, held in Medellín, Colombia, in 1968. Its "Conclusions" section has been published in the United States: *Second General Conference of Latin American Bishops: The Church in the Present-Day Transformation of Latin America in the Light of the Council* (Washington, D.C.: United States Catholic Conference, 1973).

9. "The accumulation of capital creates privileged islands within an exploited world—islands on which the most unrestrained accumulation is associated with high wages and generous social spending by First World governments. . . . The accumulation of capital is given free reign over large, impoverished regions. The population and nature are exploited, in subjection to capital. And the modern islands in that vast impoverished world are willingly subject to capital. . . . Only in this way can the legitimacy of these developed islands be established on a broad enough base to enable some of them to maintain parliamentary governments. Elsewhere recourse is made to governments based on force, which could not survive without the backing that First World countries (which are democratically legitimized) give them." Franz Hinkelammert in Pablo Richard et al., *The Idols of Death and the God of Life* (Maryknoll, N.Y.: Orbis, 1983), p. 189.

10. On the origin and background of the new theology among Latin American Protestants, see Mortimer Arias, "El itinerario protestante hacia una teología de la liberación," *Vida y pensamiento* 8 (1988), pp. 49–59.

11. There are many instances of this new ecumenism. Most significant is the founding of the Latin American Council of Churches (CLAI) and its ongoing dialogue with a number of Catholic bodies. Important joint work is also being done through the Commission on the History of the Church in Latin America (CEHILA). The joint Catholic-Protestant publications in recent years are numberless.

12. Probably the most significant attacks have been those of the Sacred Congregation for the Doctrine of the Faith (the successor of the ancient Inquisition), published in *L'Osservatore Romano* on Sept. 9, 1984, and April 13, 1986. On these two "findings," see Luis N. Rivera-Pagán, "El Vaticano y la teología de la liberación," *Apuntes* 6 (1986), pp. 51–60.

13. As a footnote to that story, in the fall of 1987 my wife and I were traveling through Spain when we decided to make a detour to find the little town whose story had long fascinated me. We found it at the end of a narrow, winding road, perched amid the mountains of southern Spain. By the roadside, as we approached the town, an elderly man tended a flock of sheep. We stopped to chat with him, and it was apparent that he was barely literate and had no

idea who Lope de Vega was. However, when I asked him, "Is this the famous Fuenteovejuna?" he stood erect and said in a clear, strong voice, "Todos a una." I then leaned closer to him and told him, "It's been a long time, and I won't tell anyone. Could you please tell me, ¿Quién mató al comendador?" He looked around furtively, put his hand to his mouth as if to whisper a secret, and then with a glimmer in his eye he proclaimed proudly, "Fuenteovejuna, Señor."

Chapter 2

1. A personal note may be of interest here and serve to illustrate the complex history of Hispanics in the United States. A few years ago, my brother was doing research in the Archivo de Indias in Seville when he decided during some of his spare time to inquire about the origins of my paternal grand-mother's family, who were among the founders of the town of Jaruco, Cuba. Much to his surprise, he found that they had owned land near Appalachicola, Florida, and had gone to Cuba as refugees when Florida was ceded to England as a result of the Treaty of Paris (1763).

2. In a speech on May 25, 1836 (Washington, D.C.: Gales and Seaton, 1838), p. 119.

3. "The Southern rebellion was largely the outgrowth of the Mexican War. Nations, like individuals, are punished for their transgressions. We got our punishment in the most sanguinary and expensive war of modern times." Quoted in William S. McFeely, *Grant: A Biography* (New York: W. W. Norton, 1981), p. 31.

4. I have recently been editing a history of Hispanic Methodism (*Each in Our Own Tongue*, to be published jointly by the General Commission on Archives and History and the United Methodist Publishing House). In the course of that history, one sees that the churches that eventually joined to form the United Methodist Church often planned for their mission among Hispanics on the basis of what they had learned from their work among other immigrant groups. Indeed, there were times and places where there was a single effort addressed jointly to Mexicans, Italians, and Portuguese. Needless to say, the strategies of assimilation developed under such an approach bore little fruit.

5. The same is true when it comes to ecclesiastical matters. In my own United Methodist denomination, the jurisdictional system has resulted in the detriment of Hispanic causes. In this system, the nation is divided into Juris-dictions, whose main function is to elect bishops. The system, originally devised as a way to qualm the fears of the South that its traditional ways would be overturned by the rest of the church, particularly in the election of black bishops, has divided United Methodist Hispanics. There are two Hispanic Annual Conferences, one in the South Central and another in the Northeastern Jurisdiction. There are also strong concentrations of Hispanics in every other Jurisdiction. Yet precisely as a result of the jurisdictional system, it was not until 1984 that the first—and only—Hispanic United Methodist bishop was elected.

6. U.S. Department of Commerce, Census Bureau, *Conditions of Hispanics in America Today* (Washington, D.C.: U.S. Government Printing Office, 1983),

p. 13. This document, apparently in an attempt to reduce the contrast between the economic status of Hispanics and that of whites, always compares Hispanics with "the rest of the population," which includes Afro- and Native Americans.

7. Center on Budget and Policy Priorities, Washington, D.C., news release, Sept. 2, 1986.

8. *Conditions of Hispanics*, p. 11.

9. Ibid., p. 7.

10. W. A. Díaz, *Hispanics: Challenges and Opportunities—A Working Paper from the Ford Foundation* (New York: Ford Foundation, 1984), p. 28.

11. W. L. Baumgaertner, ed., *Fact Book on Theological Education 1985–86* (Vandalia, Ohio: Association of Theological Schools, 1986), table F-4, p. 104.

12. W. L. Baumgaertner, ed., *Fact Book on Theological Education 1987–88* (Vandalia, Ohio: Association of Theological Schools, 1988), table F-4, p. 105.

13. Ibid., pp. 17, 19.

14. For instance, in the cover story of *Time* magazine, Oct. 16, 1978: "Hispanic Americans, Soon the Biggest Minority."

15. The debate over "bilingual education" has confused the goal of mainstreaming students whose native language is not English with true bilingual education. What most often passes as such is not truly bilingual education but simply a remedial program designed to help students whose native tongue is not English to join their English-speaking peers in the classroom. This is a worthy goal, but it is remedial, not bilingual, education. True bilingual education seeks to produce pupils who can function in two languages. To call remedial programs "bilingual education" is to foster the notion that bilingualism is a handicap rather than an asset, and that the goal of an educated person is to forget other languages and be able to function solely in English.

16. *The Annals of America*, 20 vols. (Chicago: Encyclopaedia Brittanica, 1968).

17. A study of terms such as "America" and "Americanism," their use in both English and Spanish, and the manner in which such use has evolved would provide interesting insights into the ideological shifts of the twentieth century. In Latin America, in the early postwar years, "América" was a continent in which we all shared—or so we thought—and "Panamericanismo" was the commitment of the American republics to support one another and their democratic institutions. There was even a "Panamerican hymn," sung in school functions throughout Latin America. Today, there is little talk of "Panamerican ideals" in Latin America, and what remains is considered only a relic of the past.

18. A curious twist is that even when the Spanish language is taught in U.S. schools, it is done in a way that is demeaning to Hispanics. Just about the first thing students are told is that there are two sorts of Spanish: "Castillian" and "Latin American Spanish." The implication is that what is spoken in Latin America is a corruption of proper Spanish. The fact of the matter is that the official name of the language, on both sides of the Atlantic, is "castellano"; there are other Spanish languages, such as Gallician and Catalonian, that are indeed separate languages, with their own grammars and literatures. A further fact is

that the differences between the two forms of castellano are probably not as marked as the differences between British and American English (for instance, there is no such thing as a "Latin American spelling," but there is an "American spelling"). And a final fact is that in Spain itself there are millions who speak what in the United States is called "Latin American Spanish." One suspects, then, that the real reason for the exaggerated distinction is to make it possible to study Spanish as a literary language—after all, Spain too is part of European tradition!—without having to deal with the actual people who speak that language in our own communities.

19. A point poignantly made by Rodolfo Gonzales in *Yo soy Joaquín: An Epic Poem* (New York: Bantam, 1967).

20. See Renny Golden and Michael McConnell, *Sanctuary: The New Underground Railroad* (Maryknoll, N.Y.: Orbis, 1986); Rafael J. Aragón, "El movimiento de refugio," *Apuntes* 5 (1985), pp. 65–67; Fernando Santillana, "La experiencia espiritual en el trabajo de santuario," *Apuntes* 5 (1985), pp. 68–71, and "¿Refugiados económicos, o víctimas?" *Apuntes* 5 (1985), pp. 81–86.

21. It is for this reason that reflection on issues of migration play such an important role in our theological discussion. See Francisco O. García-Treto, "El Señor guarda a los emigrantes (Salmo 146:3)," *Apuntes* 1, no. 4 (1981), pp. 3–9; Jorge Lara-Braud, "Reflexiones teológicas sobre la migración," *Apuntes* 2 (1982), pp. 3–7; Hugo L. López, "Toward a Theology of Migration," *Apuntes* 2 (1982), pp. 68–71, and "El Divino Migrante," *Apuntes* 4 (1984), pp. 14–19.

Chapter 3

1. For this reason, the title of Richard Shaull's book on the subject is particularly appropriate: *Heralds of a New Reformation: The Poor of South and North America* (Maryknoll, N.Y.: Orbis, 1984).

2. Irenaeus, *Adv. haer.*, i. praef.

3. I quote this development only as a example of what takes place constantly and repeatedly throughout the "underdeveloped" world. There is a poignant article on the case of the Philippines and Del Monte pineapples in Paul Brubaker, "Martial Law Pineapples," *Sojourners* (Oct. 1978), pp. 16–18.

4. On the specific issue of Hispanic women, see Ana María Isasi-Díaz, " 'Apuntes' for a Hispanic Women's Theology of Liberation," *Apuntes* 6 (1986), pp. 61–71, and "Mujeristas: A Name of Our Own," in Marc H. Ellis and Otto Maduro, eds., *The Future of Liberation Theology: Essays in Honor of Gustavo Gutiérrez* (Maryknoll, N.Y.: Orbis, 1989), pp. 410–19; Ana María Isasi-Díaz and Yolanda Tarango, *Hispanic Women: Prophetic Voices in the Church* (San Francisco: Harper & Row, 1988); Lydia Hernández, "La mujer chicana y la justicia económica," *Apuntes* 6 (1986), pp. 81–84; Pedro A. Sandín-Fremaint, "Hacia una teología feminista puertorriqueña," *Apuntes* 4 (1984), pp. 27–37.

5. The subject of Galilee as a paradigm for Hispanic-American theology has been explored by Virgilio Elizondo, *Galilean Journey: The Mexican-American Promise* (Maryknoll, N.Y.: Orbis, 1983), and by Orlando E. Costas, "Evangelism from the Periphery: A Galilean Model," *Apuntes* 2 (1982), pp. 51–59, and

"Evangelism from the Periphery: The Universality of Galilee," *Apuntes* 2 (1982), pp. 75–84.

6. *Heidelberg Disputation,* thesis 21. Cf. W. V. Loewenich, *Luther's Theologia Crucis* (Munich: Kaiser Verlag, 1954).

7. This is a common theme in Latin American liberation theology. Samuel Soliván, formerly of New York Theological Seminary and currently at Andover Newton Theological School, is working on the theme of "orthopathos" as a necessary element in every theology and a particularly important contribution of Hispanic-American experience.

8. In *Christian Thought Revisited: Three Types of Theology* (Nashville: Abingdon, 1989) I have spelled this out more fully. Briefly, the root of the problem is that both Roman Catholic and Protestant orthodoxies are instances of a single type of theology, one that was not the dominant type in the early church, and one in which sin and salvation are understood in terms of law, debt, and payment.

9. Ernesto Cardenal, *The Gospel in Solentiname,* 3 vols. (Maryknoll, N.Y.: Orbis, 1976–1982).

Chapter 4

1. *Inter caetera, Eximiae devotionis,* second *Inter caetera, Piis fidelium,* and *Duum siquidem.* These are to be found in the extensive work by F. J. Hernáez, *Colección de bulas, breves y otros documentos relativos a la iglesia de América y Filipinas,* 2 vols. (Brussels, 1879; Vaduz: Kraus Reprint, 1964). On the background of these bulls, both in Portuguese missions and in the Crusades, see F. Mateos, "Bulas portuguesas y españolas sobre descubrimientos geográficos," *Missionalia Hispanica* 19 (1962), pp. 5–34, 129–68. There has been considerable debate as to the reasons why these bulls were issued and what their original intent and scope were. See M. Giménez Fernández, *Nuevas consideraciones sobre la historia y sentido de las bulas alejandrinas de 1943 referentes a las Indias* (Seville: Anuario de estudios americanos, 1944), and "Todavía más sobre las letras alejandrinas de 1493 referentes a las Indias," *Anales de la Universidad Hispalense* 14 (1953), pp. 241–301. The other main participant in the controversy was V. D. Sierra, "En torno a las bulas alejandrinas de 1493," *Missionalia Hispanica* 10 (1953), pp. 73–122, and "Y nada más sobre las bulas alejandrinas de 1493," *Missionalia Hispanica* 12 (1955), pp. 403–28. On the basis for the bulls on the legal theory of the time, see P. Castañeda, "Las bulas alejandrinas y la extensión del poder indirecto," *Missionalia Hispanica* 28 (1971), pp. 215–48.

2. The year 1501 is the date of Alexander's bull to this effect. Yet the tone of the bull itself, as well as other signs, would seem to indicate that by then this was already established practice. The bull is in Hernáez, *Colección de bulas,* vol. 1, pp. 20–21.

3. At least during the early stages of the conquest, the crown did not profit directly from this arrangement, for two-thirds of such income was used to support the work of the Church, and the rest was employed in works of charity.

F. X. Montalbán, *Manual de historia de las misiones* (Bilbao: El Siglo de las Misiones, 1961), pp. 256–58.

4. Bull *Universalis ecclesiae*, 1508, in Hernáez, *Collección de bulas*, vol.1, pp. 24–25.

5. See A. de Egaña, *La teoría del regio vicariato español en Indias* (Rome: Universitas Gregoriana, 1958). This includes an extensive bibliography on the subject, on pp. xi-xx.

6. This was already apparent in Isabella's oft-quoted words, spoken upon hearing that Columbus had sent to Spain some Indians to sell as slaves: "Who has given the Admiral the right to sell my subjects?" Isabella ordered that any who had bought such Indians must return them to their land of origin, under penalty of death. A. de Herrera y Tordesillas, *Historia general de los hechos de los castellanos en las islas y tierra firme del mar Océano*, 4 vols. (Madrid, 1601), vol. 1, p. 256. Similar attitudes appeared throughout the early decades of the conquest, until Spanish power was firmly entrenched, not only over the Indians but also and especially over the conquistadors and their descendants. This is not to say, however, that moral considerations did not enter into the picture. Isabella herself was personally concerned over the well-being of her Indian subjects—to the point of issuing instructions that they should not bathe so often. And Charles V, partially as a result of the writings of Las Casas and Vitoria, for a time considered abandoning the entire enterprise as morally unjustifiable. However, economic and political considerations prevailed, and the enterprise continued. The classical work on this entire issue is L. Hanke, *The Spanish Struggle for Justice in the Conquest of America* (Philadelphia: University of Pennsylvania Press, 1949). See also L. B. Simpson, *Los conquistadores y el indio americano* (Barcelona: Ediciones Península, 1970).

7. The most remarkable exception is Las Casas, who was made bishop of Chiapas after he had become well known in government circles for his advocacy for the Indians.

8. See C. Bayle, *El clero secular y la evangelización de América* (Madrid: Consejo Superior de Investigaciones Científicas, 1950).

9. The bibliography on the Franciscans in the Spanish colonies is immense. Much of it is listed in or can be traced through Pedro Borges, *Métodos misionales en la cristianización de América* (Madrid: Consejo Superior de Investigaciones Científicas, 1960), pp. 12–13.

10. A. Figueras, "Principios de la expansión dominicana en Indias," *Missionalia Hispanica* 1 (1944), pp. 303–40.

11. F. Mateos, "Antecedentes de la entrada de los jesuitas españoles en las misiones de América," *Missionalia Hispanica* 1 (1944), pp. 106–66, and "Primera expedición de misioneros jesuitas al Perú," *Missionalia Hispanica* 2 (1945), pp. 41–108.

12. J. Castro Seoane, "La expansión de la Merced en la América colonial," *Missionalia Hispanica* 1 (1944), pp. 73–108; 2 (1945), pp. 231–30; J. Castro Seoane, "La Merced en el Perú," *Missionalia Hispanica* 3 (1946), pp. 243–320; 4 (1947), pp. 137–69, 383–401; 7 (1950), pp. 55–80.

NOTES TO PAGES 58–61

13. Lewis Hanke, *Las teorías políticas de Bartolomé de Las Casas* (Buenos Aires: J. Peuser, 1935); Henry Raup Wagner, *The Life and Writings of Bartolomé de Las Casas* (Albuquerque: University of New Mexico Press, 1967); Angel Losada, *Fray Bartolomé de Las Casas a la luz de la moderna crítica histórica* (Madrid: Tecnos, 1970); Juan Friede and Benjamin Keen, *Bartolomé de Las Casas in History: Toward an Understanding of the Man and His Work* (DeKalb, Ill.: Northern Illinois University Press, 1971); Lewis Hanke, *All Mankind Is One: A Study of the Disputation between Bartolomé de Las Casas and Juan Ginés de Sepúlveda in 1550 on the Intellectual and Religious Capacity of the American Indians* (DeKalb, Ill.: Northern Illinois University Press, 1974); Comisión de Estudios de Historia de la Iglesia en Latinoamérica (CEHILA), *Bartolomé de Las Casas (1474–1974) e historia de la iglesia en América Latina* (Barcelona: Terra Nova, 1976); Juan Friede, *Bartolomé de Las Casas, precursor del anticolonialismo: Su lucha y su derrota* (México: Siglo Veintiuno, 1976); Ramón-Jesús Queralto Moreno, *El pensamiento filosófico-político de Bartolomé de Las Casas* (Sevilla: Escuela de Estudios Hispano-Americanos, 1976).

14. Alvaro Sánchez, *El Apóstol del Nuevo Reino: San Luis Beltrán* (Bogotá: Santafé, 1953). At a more popular level: Stephen Clissold, *The Saints of South America* (London: Charles Knight & Co., 1972), pp. 12–29.

15. The most complete history of the Jesuit missions in Paraguay, especially valuable for its collection of primary sources, is Pablo Pastells, *Historia de la Compañia de Jesús en la Provincia del Paraguay*, 8 vols. (Madrid: V. Suárez, 1912–1949). See also M. Mörner, *The Political and Economic Activities of the Jesuits in the La Plata Region: The Hapsburg Era* (Stockholm: Victor Pettersons Bokindustri Artiebolag, 1953); F. Mateos, "La Guerra Guaranítica y las misiones del Paraguay," *Missionalia Hispanica* 8 (1951), pp. 241–316; 9 (1952), pp. 75–121.

16. Antonio de Egaña, *Historia de la Iglesia en América Española: Desde el Descubrimiento hasta comienzos del siglo XIX*, vol. 2, *Hemisferio sur* (Madrid: Biblioteca de Autores Cristianos, 1966), p. 209. Egaña himself is not very sympathetic toward Gil González.

17. Mariano Picón Salas, *Pedro Claver: El santo de los esclavos* (Mexico: Fondo de Cultura Económica, 1949); Angel Valtierra, *Peter Claver: Saint of the Slaves* (London: Burns & Oates, 1960). A brief biography: Clissold, *The Saints*, pp. 173–201.

18. Quoted by Boleslao Lewin, *La rebelión de Túpac Amaru* (Buenos Aires: Sociedad Editora Latino Americana, 1967), p. 503.

19. It is also to be noted that the Virgin of Copacabana played a similar role in some sectors of the Túpac Amaru rebellion.

20. The sources from which the various steps in the legend, as well as the development of the legend itself, may be reconstructed may be found in León Lopetegui and Félix Zubillaga, *Historia de la Iglesia en América española: Desde el descubrimiento hasta comienzos del siglo XIX*, vol. 1, *México. América Central. Antillas* (Madrid: Biblioteca de Autores Cristianos, 1955), pp. 345–54.

21. This is why the Virgin of Guadalupe plays such an important role in Catholic Mexican-American theology. See Andrés Gonzales Guerrero, *A Chicano Theology* (Maryknoll, N.Y.: Orbis, 1987); Virgilio Elizondo, *La morenita:*

Evangelizadora de las Américas (Liguori, Mo.: Liguori Publications, 1981); Eduardo Hoornaert, "La evangelización según la tradición guadalupana," in SELADOC, *Religiosidad popular* (Salamanca: Sígueme, 1976), pp. 260–79.

22. Carlos Rosas, one of the foremost Hispanic hymnologists in the country, a faithful Catholic and choir director in San Antonio, has expressed such feelings in a song that has become quite popular, "El profeta del barrio." After an initial stanza about Jesus preaching in Galilee and the people's response, the chorus says: "Es hijo del carpintero. / Profeta no puede ser. / Es uno de nuestro barrio. / Profeta no puede ser." (He is the carpenter's son. / A prophet he cannot be. / He is one of our very own. / A prophet he cannot be.) The third, fourth, and fifth stanzas, in a rough translation, say: "The Virgin looked upon Juan Diego with loving eyes; but the bishop was blind and thus he did not believe. What happened to Juan Diego also happens to many now; Juan Diego was not of the clergy, and the bishop did not believe. The wise and the learned misjudge the poor; they look upon them as retarded and try to keep them down."

23. See Dora Ortiz Vásquez, *Enchanted Temples of Taos* (Santa Fe: Rydal Press, 1975). Ms. Ortiz Vásquez is a great-granddaughter of Fr. Martínez.

24. There are at the time of this writing two Hispanic archbishops (San Antonio and Santa Fe), six diocesan bishops (Fresno, Tucson, El Paso, Corpus Christi, Las Cruces, and Pueblo), and eleven auxiliary bishops (Newark, Los Angeles [2], San Diego, Washington, Sacramento, Houston, New York, Chicago, Miami, and Brooklyn). There are a total of 1,954 Hispanic priests in the United States. This does not count Puerto Rico, where the archbishop and the hierarchy are Puerto Ricans. Manuel J. Rodríguez, ed., *Directorio de sacerdotes hispanos en los Estados Unidos de América* (Forest Hills, N.Y.: Herencia española, 1986). Information updated by the Secretariat for Hispanic Affairs.

25. Secretariat for Hispanic Affairs, *Proceedings of the II Encuentro Nacional Hispano de Pastoral* (Washington, D.C.: National Catholic Conference, 1977), p. 25.

26. Ibid., p. 28.

27. Secretariat for Hispanic Affairs, *Pueblo Hispano—Voz Profética* (Washington, D.C.: National Catholic Conference, 1985), p. 77.

28. Ibid., p. 76.

29. Ibid., p. 125.

30. *L'impérialisme protestant: Considérations sur le destin inégal des peuples protestants et catholiques dans le monde actuel* (Paris: Flammarion, 1948).

31. On the life and work of Thomson, see J. C. Varetto, *Diego Thomson* (Buenos Aires: La Aurora, 1918).

32. Bolívar and several of the principal leaders of Latin American independence believed that the traditions of authoritarianism and obscurantism were so ingrained in the entire continent that democracy would only be possible if those traditions were broken. For a time, Bolívar considered the advisability of placing the entire continent under the temporary tutelage of Great Britain. He also hoped that the United States would support his efforts toward a unified and democratic Hispanic America. The policies of the United

States to scuttle such attempts at unity at the Panama Congress were a deep disappointment to Bolívar and to many of his generation. In any case, the policy of most of the young republics was to foster immigration from Europe, especially from the North Atlantic, in the hope of bringing in new industries, opening up land for agriculture, and introducing traditions of democratic government.

33. As far as is known, the first Protestant sermons in Spanish in Argentina and in Uruguay were preached by Scotsman John F. Thomson, a member of the immigrant community. See J. C. Varetto, *El apóstol del Plata: Juan F. Thomson* (Buenos Aires: La Aurora, 1943).

34. I have written a summary of this process for Episcopalians, Presbyterians, and Methodists in *The Development of Christianity in the Latin Caribbean* (Grand Rapids, Mich.: Eerdmans, 1969), pp. 91–95.

35. T. S. Goslin, *Los evangélicos en la América Latina* (Buenos Aires: La Aurora, 1956), pp. 95, 103.

36. For two different and often conflicting evaluations, specifically on the case of Chile, compare Christian Lalive d'Epinay, *El refugio de las masas: Estudio sociológico del protestantismo chileno* (Santiago de Chile: Editorial del Pacífico, 1968), with Emilio Willems, *Followers of the New Faith: Culture Change and the Rise of Protestantism in Brazil and Chile* (Nashville: Vanderbilt University Press, 1967).

37. In more recent years, a new wave of Pentecostalism and fundamentalism has been added. This is closely connected both with the "electronic church" and with the New Right in the United States and has been particularly successful in Mexico and Central America—Guatemala above all. With very significant financial support from elements in the United States that fear the spread of revolutionary sentiments in Central America, the message of this new form of Protestantism is as otherworldly as that of any previous form. The dimension that is now added, however, is that the great apostasy both of Roman Catholicism and of many Protestant bodies is their involvement in matters of this world. While in earlier times the Catholic "heresy" was "popery," now the heresies are liberation theology, Christian Base Communities, and any form of political involvement. On these items, they are virulently anti-Catholic. Given the present situation, particularly in countries such as Guatemala, where death squads have killed hundreds of Catholic lay catechists and Base Community organizers, this is resulting in unprecedented religious and political tensions. These "new" Protestants claim to stay out of politics, but in fact they support the status quo and say and do nothing about the abuses committed against those who seek political and social changes. Thus it is to be feared that if such changes ever come, they will be followed by painful reprisals, and many in the United States who said nothing about the death squads will cry foul.

Chapter 5

1. The place of this and similar traditions in the biblical view of history has been explored by Susan Niditch, *Underdogs and Tricksters: A Prelude to Biblical Folklore* (San Francisco: Harper & Row, 1987).

2. *The Tribes of Yahweh: A Sociology of the Religion of Liberated Israel, 1250–1050 B.C.E.* (Maryknoll: Orbis, 1979), p. 11.

3. A summary of the manner in which the Old Roman Symbol, the forerunner of the Apostles' Creed, responded to Marcionism may be found in Justo L. González, *A History of Christian Thought*, 2nd ed., vol. 1 (Nashville: Abingdon, 1987), pp. 151–54.

4. In Spanish, we call the Older Testament "el Antiguo Testamento." The word "antiguo," unlike "old," does not necessarily have the connotation of being outdated or surpassed. It may be applied to customs or traditions that have value precisely because of their antiquity.

5. An excellent and concise discussion of how this reading takes place, for those who are not acquainted with it firsthand, is Carlos Mesters, "The Use of the Bible in Christian Communities of Common People," in Sergio Torres and John Eagleson, eds., *The Challenge of Basic Christian Communities* (Maryknoll, N.Y.: Orbis, 1981), pp. 197–210. Two paragraphs in this article are worth quoting: "Biblical exegetes, using their heads and their studies, can come fairly close to Abraham; but their feet are a long way from Abraham. The common people are very close to Abraham with their feet. They are living the same sort of situation. Their life-process is of the same nature and they can identify with him. When they read his story in the Bible, it becomes a mirror for them" (p. 203); "At one session we were reading the following text: 'I have heard the cries of my people.' A woman who worked in a factory offered this commentary: 'The Bible does not say that God has heard the praying of the people. It says that God has heard the cries of his people. I don't mean that people shouldn't pray. I mean that people should imitate God. Very often we work to get people to go to church and pray first; and only then will we pay heed to their cries' " (p. 207).

6. J. L. González and C. G. González, *Liberation Preaching: The Pulpit and the Oppressed* (Nashville: Abingdon, 1980), pp. 69–93.

7. And in three of these cases—the "Pastoral Epistles"—most scholars agree that they were not written singly to either Timothy or Titus and that therefore the singular "you" is a literary device in writings that in truth are addressed to the church at large.

Chapter 6

1. *Apol.* 3. 2.

2. In spite of all that has been written since, no discussion of analogy as a means of speaking about God surpasses that of Thomas Aquinas: *Summa Theol.* Ia, q. 13. See H. Lyttkens, *The Analogy Between God and the Word: An Investigation of Its Background and Interpretation of Its Use by Thomas of Aquino* (Uppsala: Almquist & Wiksells, 1952).

3. *Epid.* 22; *Adv. haer.* 3. 22. 3; 5. 16. 2.

4. *De fide orth.* 1. 16.

5. This was in essence Tertullian's response to Praxeas, who argued that his form of monarchianism was logically admissible because, after all, God is

omnipotent. See my article: "Athens and Jerusalem Revisited: Reason and Authority in Tertullian," *Church History* 43 (1974), pp. 17–25.

6. Unfortunately, the Latin translation, lacking a better word, says "omnipotens," which can indeed be understood as an affirmation of the unlimited power of God.

7. Although it has become customary to translate the Creed as speaking of a "Father" almighty, the structure of the Greek language—specifically, the manner in which Greek uses gender—makes the translation "Parent" equally valid.

8. *Strom.* 2. 16.

Chapter 7

1. "In putting the doctrine of the Trinity at the head of the whole of dogmatics we are adopting a position which, looked at in view of the history of dogmatics, is very isolated. Still, not quite isolated: in the Middle Ages it was Peter Lombard in his *Sentences* and Bonaventura in his *Breviloquium*, who likewise took up this attitude." *Church Dogmatics* (Edinburgh: T & T Clark, 1936), I/1, p. 345.

2. For instance, Clement, *Ad Cor.* 46. 6; 58. 2.

3. *II Clem.* 15. 1; *Ascension of Isaiah* 10. 4. Cf. Jean Daniélou, "Trinité et angélologie dans la théologie judéo-chrétienne," *Recherches de Science Religieuse* 45 (1957), pp. 5–41.

4. This is an image characteristic of Irenaeus. See Jean Mambrino, "Les *Deux Mains de Dieu* dans l'oeuvre de saint Irenée," *Nouvelle Revue Théologique* 79 (1957), pp. 355–70. I have discussed the significance of this image in *Christian Thought Revisited*, p. 45.

5. Justin, *I Apol.* 46. 3–4; *II Apol.* 7. 3; 10. 2–3.

6. The critical edition of *Fonti Ricciane* is currently being published (Rome: Libreria do Bello Stato, 1942–). Two good introductions are V. Cronin, *The Wise Man from the West* (London: R. Hart-Davis, 1955), and George H. Dunne, *Generation of Giants: The Story of the Jesuits in China in the Last Decades of the Ming Dynasty* (London: Burns & Oates, 1962). On the theological issues involved, see J. Bettray, *Die Akommodationsmethode des P. Matteo Ricci in China* (Rome: Universitas Gregoriana, 1955). I have summarized the controversy over Ricci's methods and their results in *The Story of Christianity*, vol. 1 (San Francisco: Harper & Row, 1984), pp. 407–9. On de Nobili, see V. Cronin, *A Pearl to India: The Life of Roberto de Nobili* (New York: E. P. Dutton, 1959).

7. The debate as to whether the American Indians were fully human had to do with more than the possibility of their conversion. It also involved their rights to own and manage property, and, in the church, the possibility of their ordination. The theory that the native inhabitants of these lands were, at best, "like children" was the basis not only for much well-intentioned paternalism but also for the expropriation of lands and various other forms of exploitation. And the theory still lingers. In the twentieth century a Spanish Catholic historian, after agreeing that the false sense of superiority of the early Spanish

missionaries did much damage, goes on to say, "Anyone who knows anything about América [meaning the Western Hemisphere] realizes that some tribes that have been isolated from all civilized life need some time to assimilate the principles of a higher level of human life." León Lopetegui in León Lopetegui and Félix Zubillaga, *Historia de la Iglesia en América española: Desde el descubrimiento hasta comienzos del siglo XIX*, vol. 1, *México. América Central. Antillas* (Madrid: Biblioteca de Autores Cristianos, 1955), p. 100.

8. *Dial.* 56. 11.

9. All of this is not to ignore or reject the very convincing argument of R. C. Gregg and D. E. Groh that the issues involved in the early stages of the debate were essentially soteriological; Gregg and Groh, *Early Arianism: A View of Salvation* (Philadelphia: Fortress Press, 1981). Still, out of various soteriological concerns, the debate revolved around the divinity of the Word.

10. *On the Duties of Ministers* 1. 28. 132.

11. *Ep.* 120.

12. *Hom.* 2. 3.

13. *Hom.* 14. 26. These are only a few of hundreds of quotations that could be adduced. I have included many more in *Faith and Wealth: A History of Early Christian Ideas on the Origin, Significance and Use of Money* (San Francisco: Harper & Row, 1990).

14. This was already seen by Adolph Harnack, whose comments on the Nicene formula and its use are very much to the point: "The victory of the Nicene Creed was a victory of the priests over the faith of the Christian people. The Logos-doctrine had already become unintelligible to those who were not theologians. . . . The thought that Christianity is the revelation of something incomprehensible became more and more familiar to men's minds. . . It is alarming to note in the ecclesiastical literature of the Fourth Century and the period following how little attention is given to the Christian *people*. . . . The people must simply believe the Faith; they accordingly did not live in this Faith, but in that Christianity of the second rank which is represented in the legends of the saints, in apocalypses, in image-worship." *History of Dogma*, vol. 4 (New York: Russell & Russell, 1958), pp. 106–7.

15. The following report by Eldridge Cleaver, tragic in its simplicity, needs no comment: "It all ended one day when, at a catechism class, the priest asked if anyone understood the mystery of the Holy Trinity. I had been studying my lessons diligently and knew by heart what I'd been taught. Up shot my hand, my heart throbbing with piety (pride) for this chance to demonstrate my knowledge of the Word. To my great shock and embarrassment, the Father announced, and it sounded like a thunderclap, that I was lying, that no one, not even the Pope, understood the Godhead, and why else did I think they called it the *mystery* of the Holy Trinity? I saw in a flash, stung to the quick by the jeers of my fellow catechumens, that I had been used." *Soul on Ice*, (New York: Dell, 1968), p. 31.

16. In G. H. Anderson and T. F. Stransky, eds., *Mission Trends No. 3: Third World Theologies* (New York: Paulist Press, 1976), pp. 151–2.

17. *Adv. Prax.* 4.

18. Ibid., 3.
19. *Apol.* 39.

Chapter 8

1. "Heaven is the creation inconceivable to man; earth is the creation conceivable to him. . . . This entire 'beyond' which is withdrawn from man and confronts him, in part menacingly, in part gloriously, must not of course be confused with God. When we have reached what to us is inconceivable, we have not reached God, but merely heaven. If we wanted to call this inconceivable reality God, we should be playing at deification of the creature no less than when so-called 'primitive man' worships the sun. Very many philosophers have been guilty of such deification of the creature. The boundary of our conceiving is not the boundary that separates us from God, but solely the boundary which the Creed calls the boundary between heaven and earth." Karl Barth, *Dogmatics in Outline* (New York: Harper & Brothers, 1959), pp. 61–62.

2. *Kerygma and Myth* (New York: Harper & Row, 1961), p. 5.

3. Almost since the beginning of my theological studies, I have been very much influenced by José Ortega y Gasset and his understanding of reason. Particularly helpful is his article "Ni vitalismo ni racionalismo," published in the October 1924 issue of *Revista de Occidente* and reprinted in José Ortega y Gasset, *Obras Completas*, vol. 3 (Madrid: Revista de Occidente, 1947), pp. 270–80.

4. A phrase borrowed from Irenaeus, who when referring to the Genesis stories usually speaks of them not as "creation" but rather as "the beginning of creation."

Chapter 9

1. H. Denzinger, *Enchiridon symbolorum definitionum et declarationum de rebus fidei et morum*, 31st ed. (Rome: Herder, 1957), pp. 165–66.

2. *Obras Completas*, vol. 6 (Madrid: Revista de Occidente, 1947), p. 32.

3. A short study on this matter, which has become a classic, is Oscar Cullmann, *Immortality of the Soul or Resurrection of the Dead? The Witness of the New Testament* (London: Epworth, 1958).

4. *Church Dogmatics* (Edinburgh: T & T Clark, 1936), III/2, p. 372.

5. Ibid., III/2, p. 419.

6. *Reges.* 1. 401.

7. Historically, there is a connection between the hierarchization of body and soul and the hierarchization of functions in society. To prove this point, it suffices to look at the third book of Plato's *Republic*, where he posits the theory that there are three races: one of gold (the philosophers, who should also be the rulers), one of silver (the warriors), and one of bronze (those who work with their hands). As to slaves, they do not deserve to be even counted among these three races.

8. Vine Deloria, Jr., *God Is Red* (New York: Dell, 1973), p. 96.

9. Thus, for instance, Lesslie Newbigin: "If we take the New Testament as our clue to the interpretation of history, then we shall see the world-wide spread of a single technological culture, propelled by the single driving force of a secularized eschatology, as something which is much more than mere scenery for the present stage of the Christian task in the world. We shall see it as part of the process by which all peoples are being brought into that single universal history which is rightly counted from the birth of Christ." *A Faith for This One World?* (London: SCM Press, 1961), pp. 28–29. Newbigin, however, does acknowledge the power that such technological development has of serving the Antichrist.

Chapter 10

1. The standard study is still that of Gustave Bardy, *Paul de Samosate: Etude historique* (Louvain: Spicilegium Sacrum Lovaniense, 1929).

2. Bonhoeffer, however, is correct in arguing that in spite of its explicit adoptionism, liberal theology is ultimately docetic, for it idealizes the historical Jesus: "Liberal theology was fond of referring to Paul of Samosata as a forerunner. True, there are analogies, but this reference to him is in fact unjustified. Liberal theology is, in its essentials, not Ebionite, but docetic in nature." *Christ the Center* (New York: Harper & Row, 1966), p. 87.

3. For a fuller discussion of the historical material that follows, see J. L. González, *A History of Christian Thought*, 2nd ed., vol. 1 (Nashville: Abingdon, 1987), pp. 335–80.

4. Indeed, when explaining the Christological controversies of the fifth century, and the various options that were condemned, I have found the image of "hot ice cream" a useful one. If asked for hot ice cream, some of the options are (1) a "baked Alaska," in which the ice cream is kept frozen by insulating it from the heat (Nestorianism?); or (2) mixing all the ingredients for ice cream and then heating them (monophysism?). At this point, some student invariably breaks in: "What about making ice cream with tabasco sauce?" Precisely! What that student has done is redefine what is meant by "hot." The problem is essentially one of definitions, and as long as we continue defining "divine" and "human" in mutually contradictory ways, the contradiction will remain.

5. *Ep.* 101 (NPNF, 2nd series, 7:440).

6. R. V. Sellers, *The Council of Chalcedon* (London: SPCK, 1953), pp. 210–11.

7. *Church Dogmatics* (Edinburgh: T & T Clark, 1936), IV/I, p. 186.

8. Ibid., IV/2, p. 353.

9. *Vida de Don Quijote y Sancho*, 14th ed. (Madrid: Espasa-Calpe, S.A., 1966), p. 12.

10. A series of lectures originally delivered at the University of Uppsala in 1930, and published in English shortly thereafter (New York: Macmillan, 1931).

11. I have tried to show this connection, as well as how these views of the work of Christ relate to other aspects of theology, in *Christian Thought Revisited: Three Types of Theology* (Nashville: Abingdon, 1989).

12. Irenaeus, *Adv. haer.* 5. preface; Athanasius, *De inc.* 54.; *Ep. ad Adelph.* 4. There may be a similar view behind II Peter 1:4.

Chapter 11

1. In my own United Methodist Church, there are a number of examples of this quest for structural solutions. One such example is James W. Holsinger and Evelyn Laycock, *Awaken the Giant: 28 Prescriptions for Reviving the United Methodist Church* (Nashville: Abingdon, 1988). The very title, "28 prescriptions," indicates the tone of the book. Essentially, what these authors feel we have to do is change the organization and establish new programs—do away with ethnic and gender quotas, have a chief executive officer, make pastors' continued employment contingent on their productivity, require courses on evangelism in seminaries, and so on. Some of these may be good suggestions; most are very bad; but in any case they do not really get at the root of the malaise.

2. As has been pointed out elsewhere, this is really what Nicodemus balks at when told that he must be born anew. To be born anew also implies to die to the old.

3. Among many other relevant passages, the following may be noted: Isaiah 65:17; 66:22. In Jeremiah 31:22 the newness of what God does is to change what people considered the established social order. This emphasis on surprising newness as a sign of the work of God is to be found not only in the prophets but throughout Scripture. See, for instance, Numbers 16:29–30, where a new and unexpected thing is declared to be a sign of God's action.

4. This has been particularly true of some elements within the Lutheran tradition, based on a partial understanding of Luther's doctrine of the "two kingdoms." On Luther's own views, see W. D. J. Cargill Thompson, *The Political Thought of Martin Luther* (Brighton, Sussex: Harvester, 1984).

5. See, for instance, Irenaeus, *Adv. haer.* 3. 19. 3 (*Ante-Nicene Fathers*, vol. 1, p. 449): Jesus "making in His own person the first-fruits of the resurrection of man; that, as the Head rose from the dead, so also the remaining part of the body—[namely the body] of every man who is found in life—when the time is fulfilled ... may arise, blended together and strengthened through joints and bands."